Dorie

Woman of the Mountains

Florence Cope Bush

With an Afterword by Durwood Dunn

UNIVERSITY OF TENNESSEE PRESS / KNOXVILLE

Photographs on pages 13, 19, 44, 84, 115, 126, 127, 167, 196, 197, 198, and 220
are printed courtesy of the Great Smoky Mountains National Park.

The paper used in this book meets the minimum requirements of ANSI/NISO
Z39.48-1992 (R 1997) (Permanence of Paper). The binding materials have been
chosen for strength and durability. Printed on recycled paper.

Library of Congress Cataloging in Publication Data

Bush, Florence Cope, 1933–
        Dorie: woman of the mountains / Florence Cope Bush:
with an afterword by Durwood Dunn.
            p.   cm.
        Includes bibliographical references.
        ISBN 0-87049-725-1 (cloth: alk. paper)
        ISBN 0-87049-726-X (pbk.: alk. paper)
        1. Cope, Dorie Woodruff. 2. Great Smoky Mountains
        (N.C. and Tenn.)—Biography. 3. Great Smoky Mountains
        (N.C. and Tenn.)—Social life and customs. 4. Mountain life—
        Great Smoky Mountains (N.C. and Tenn.)   I. Title
        CT275.C777B87   1992
        976.8'8905'092—dc20   91–12875
        [B]

Dorie

Woman of the Mountains

Contents

Illustrations

Maps

Introduction

My parents, Dorie Woodruff Cope and Fred Cope, were part of the mass migration of people leaving the mountains when the government claimed their homeland to establish the Great Smoky Mountains National Park. I was born in Tremont, a settlement between Townsend and Cades Cove. When they left their home, I was three years old, and I have no memory of ever having lived in the misty, blue mountains. But everything about the Smokies fascinates me, and I'm ever drawn back to the place of my birth.

My heart has always been in the mountains. Many summers spent with my grandparents on their farm in Sevier County, Tennessee, gave me a sense of relation to the mountains and their people. Granny and I spent evenings going through the family pictures and records she kept in a large trunk beside their bed. Even then, I felt a sense of loss because no one seemed to care about the lives these people had led, how they got to where they were, or that they even existed.

Many years after the death of my grandparents and my father, I felt the familiar urge to go home to the Smokies. Knowing we were losing a part of our heritage, I spent nine years talking to my mother, Dora (Dorie) Woodruff Cope, about her childhood and life in the mountains. Memories long forgotten surfaced as we moved backward in time. One thought led to another until we were back at the beginning of her life.

Dorie: Woman of the Mountains was not written with the idea that it would ever be published. I wrote it as a gift to my daughter, my mother, and myself. The manuscript was in my possession for fifteen years before a friend talked me into letting him publish two thousand copies in paperback for local distribution. The impact of the book surprised everyone. Dorie came to represent a female relative in almost everyone's life. So often I heard, "You wrote about my mother, my grandmother, my aunt."

Much effort went into researching the accuracy of the events described in the story. My mother and I went through letters, pictures (often having valuable, descriptive material on the back), her father's time books from the Little River Lumber Company, documents from Oconalufta Township, North Carolina, and papers written by my father. I became a familiar patron in libraries and archives in both North Carolina and Tennessee. Finally, it all came together.

With Dorie, we return to a time before the "outlanders'" civilization slipped in through the door. Meager livings came from the isolated, nearly perpendicular farms in the coves and hollows. Money was almost nonexistent, and food and clothing came from back-breaking labor on one's own land. Before Mason jars were brought into the hills, food was dried or smoked. Clothing came from sheep, flax, and cotton grown on the farm.

Great changes came with the lumbermen pouring into the mountains. As money became available to the highlanders, old customs and ideas crumbled. Centuries-old arts and crafts were abandoned for modern methods. Why weave a basket when you could buy one? Wasn't a machine-made blanket better than a handcrafted quilt? Wasn't food in tin cans better than the home-dried or home-canned variety? As must always happen, the old gave way to the new.

Now, I would like for you to meet Dorie. She probably will remind you of someone you already know and love. This is my mother, telling her story as she told it to me.

Florence Cope Bush
November 29, 1990

Dorie

Woman of the Mountains

I

1898–1907

My memory may be faulty at times, but I know this to be true. Ma and Pa did everything they could to make us happy and keep us clothed and fed with what was available to them at the time. They only had their own abilities and what the mountains provided. Some would say that was poverty, but we didn't think so. Like the Cherokee and early white settlers, they used knowledge that had been gathered since the time the area was invaded by man.

Most everything we needed for survival was there in the mountains. Ma and Pa each brought their own experience and knowledge together to form our household. Although they were Appalachian mountaineers, they came from different backgrounds. Pa was Dutch, and Ma was a fiery Scots-Irish and Catawba Indian mixture. All her ancestors had been in the mountains since they arrived in this land. In a way, she was more in harmony with the wilderness than Pa.

The times we spent together are sweet in my memory. I especially liked fall. When the leaves on the hillside began showing their full blaze of color, we knew the cold, crisp air would come down from the north and remind us to get ready for winter. And, oh, the harvest moon—at night it looked like a big ball of white ice floating in a sea of purple velvet. It shone so brightly that only a few stars were visible in its glow. From where our house sat between the mountain ranges, it looked twice the size of the moon that I see since I became older.

In the fall, Ma, Pa, and we children picked up buckeyes and gave them away. By the time the old tree by the church had dropped most of its crop, the shiny, brown seeds had shed their

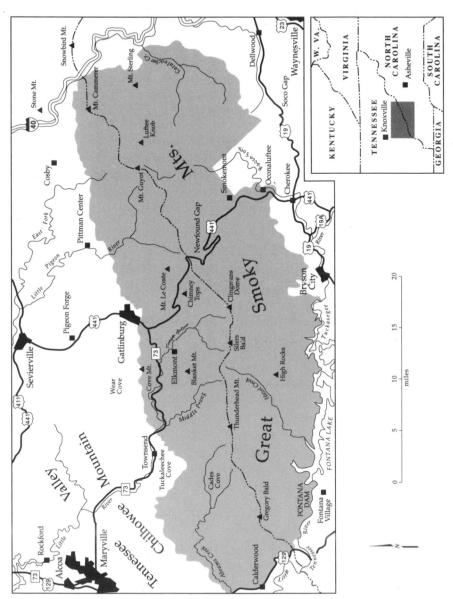

Map 1. The Great Smoky Mountains. Dorie's birthplace, Oconaluftee, North Carolina, in 1899.

rough, prickly burr husks and were waiting to be gathered. The Indians carved decorations on them to make necklaces and other kinds of jewelry out of the hard, brown shells. The only thing we did with buckeyes was give them away. They're not edible, but they make beautiful ornaments to have around the house. They were often passed down from one generation to the next. I still have my own lucky buckeye. It was Pa's and it's over a hundred years old. Courting couples sometimes opened the husks and each took one of the seeds. The buckeye is a symbol of love because two seeds fit together inside one pod— sort of like the Bible verse about marriage, where two become one.

I don't think Ma and Pa shared a buckeye. They were so different they wouldn't have fit together in one pod. I've many times wondered what attracted them to each other. Pa was so gentle and kind and one of the few men I ever saw cry. He was born in hard times in Jackson County. But then, everybody born when he was saw only hard work and sparse living in the road before them.

Pa started to work as soon as he was big enough to handle a hoe or an ax. His family saw no need for education—and, besides, it cost sixty cents a month to send your child to school. Back then, sixty cents was a lot of money. Because he couldn't read or write, he followed the timber cutters to Smokemont to work in a small sawmill. He didn't have to use his brain there, only his muscles. The hard work kept him gaunt and tired.

Maybe fate stepped in and brought him and Ma together. He wasn't handsome but he was pleasant, an upstanding young man. Being single made the local girls take notice, but he was shy. I've heard different stories about families offering him room and board or free meals if they had single daughters. Any girl would be lucky to marry him.

Ma was a beauty with boundless energy and ambition, always going and doing. She had deep blue eyes and wore her long, raven hair up in a bun on the back of her head. Fragile skin, the color of pink and white apple blossoms, covered a very strong-willed woman with a sharp wit and an equally sharp tongue. Pa always said half of the men in Swain County were afraid to speak to her because they didn't know what to do with a woman who spoke her mind. Back then, women definitely had a place, but Ma wouldn't stay in hers. She could outthink and outdo most of the men she knew.

Because she was a year older than Pa, he always said he saved her from spinsterhood by marrying her at the old age of twenty-three. If a woman wasn't married early, the only thing left for her to do was to hire herself out to do most any kind of job—even servitude. Ma had done this since she was thirteen. She went to live with families when new babies were born or when there was sickness or death. Ma helped to prepare the bodies for burial. At this time there were no funeral homes. The dead were washed, dressed in their Sunday best, and put into home-made coffins. Her pay was small, and sometimes it was trade or barter. She would accept food or cloth for payment.

Ma never said why or how she had learned to read and write. Like Pa, she never went to school, but somewhere along the way she taught herself the basics. It was easier for a woman to take a few minutes from chores to do some of the things she wanted to do. She never worked on a schedule like the men did. Ma had five sisters, and they were all very close. I know that they could all read and write because there are still letters from them in the family. Maybe, as the oldest sister, she taught the others to write, or maybe they all learned together. They shared their lives with each other through the scrawly letters they passed around until they were worn and fragile. Concerning Pa, Ma had her own plans. She had seen him at a church meeting and knew the tall, lanky man with the craggy face was the man for her. Pa must not have put up much of a fight for his bachelorhood because they married May 26, 1898. Pa's adopted father, Coleman Mills, stood up for him at the ceremony. The Reverend Alvin Beck, pastor of the church, tied the wedding knot.

Her sisters and aunts planned a wedding shivaree, but Uncle Aden talked them out of it. The boisterous celebration didn't fit his way of thinking. Or maybe he didn't want to endure the noisy festivities. The women banged the bottoms of pots and pans and marched around the bride. The groom was hoisted onto a log and carried around the house while the men teased him about getting caught by some woman. After the demonstration was over, they all went to the tables laden with desserts and coffee. The stack cake sitting in the middle of the table was the center of attention. Each lady attending the wedding had brought a layer to add to the cake. The filling was made from apples and molasses. The higher the cake, the more prominent and well known the bride.

Uncle Aden said, "Why would you want to celebrate when you have just got yourself into trouble by getting wed?" With Uncle Aden, you couldn't tell if he was joking or not. My great uncle was a very strong, opinionated man. He was a Democrat through and through, but somehow he tolerated Pa's Republican political convictions. We shouldn't have been surprised that Uncle Aden lived to be 101 years old. He had the determination to do it. Still, for all his gruffness, he was the most beloved member of the family. He believed in the rightness of the Baptist faith and practiced it. Everything he did was measured by the Golden Rule—do unto others as you would have them do unto you.

Some of his beliefs must have influenced Ma. One of her first goals was to teach Pa to read and write. He refused to go buy the big, red tablet and pencil. Ma got out her old slate and chalk to get him started. It wasn't long before she knew he needed the paper and pencil. With the slate, you write and erase constantly. She went to the store in Whittier to make the purchase and returned with more determination than before to make it work. They sat at a table he had made, in a chair he had made, and worked on letters and numerals he could barely scratch out. But finally he learned to read and write and do arith-

Aden Andrew Carver, Dorie's great-uncle, was a millwright, carpenter, and farmer. This picture was taken near his one-hundredth birthday.

metic on his own. One day in the future his skills would help him in building railroad trestles across the mountains in Tennessee.

To show his grudging gratitude, he wrote Ma a poem in his imperfect handwriting:

I do not rite fer joy
I do not rite fer fam (e)
I rite because I love you
And you holp me spell my name
[signed] R. V. Woodruff 1899

She kept it neatly folded, wrapped in a lacy handkerchief, in the big family trunk. Pa was a proud man and she knew it had been difficult for him to submit to her wishes. In her own way, she returned the favor by being a good listener.

Pa could talk for hours about his father and how he came to the Smokies and how his parents gave him the name of a Confederate general. Pa's father came from Georgia during the Civil War and had served under the command of Robert B. Vance, one of North Carolina's favorite sons. But Pa never knew his father. He died of pneumonia in December before Pa was born in February. His mother had been given an order to name the baby Robert Vance if it happened to be a boy.

Dorie: Woman of the Mountains

The Woodruff family was Black Dutch. We never learned where they came from, but it's a term everybody in the mountains knows and identifies with tall, angular featured people like Pa and Abraham Lincoln.

Pa and Ma believed the story about Abraham Lincoln being the son of Abraham Enloe, a man who lived in the same area that they came from. As the story goes, Nancy Hanks, an orphan girl, was a worker in the Enloe household and became pregnant. She ran away to Kentucky where she married Thomas Lincoln and gave birth to Abraham's child. It never seemed to bother them that history did not agree with the story. To them, Abraham Lincoln was an Enloe and Black Dutch. Some stories are too good to give up—and, besides, Pa enjoyed looking like the president. I can't say if that is why he was a life-long Republican or not.

Whatever troubles their different personalities caused were solved once they were married. They worked too hard to have enough energy left to argue. There wasn't time to dwell on slights, real or imagined. Their time together was to last forty-eight years.

Their first home was a one-room log cabin beside the Oconaluftee River. The rough cabin had a large fireplace used for both heating and cooking. The inside of the cabin was about fifteen by eighteen feet. Their only cooking utensils were a Dutch oven and a kettle or pot. An iron crane was fastened on hinges on one side of the fireplace so it could swing over the fire. The kettle hung from this crane on chains or hooks. Roasting and baking were done in the Dutch oven, which had a cast-iron lid turned up all around so that it could hold live coals of fire to heat the top and bake evenly.

Pa made their furniture. Rough lumber, hewn smooth on one side, was used for a table. Chairs were made from maple limbs, bent and coaxed into shape. Ma used thin white oak splits for weaving the seats. In the other corner of the room, a double bed with a straw tick mattress filled most of the space. They didn't have springs on the bed. Pa used rope to make the bottom. They hung their clothing on nails driven into the wall. Everything else was folded and neatly stacked on shelves along the wall.

Ma had made quilts and unbleached muslin sheets. When they were quite young, mountain girls started making quilts for their "hope chests" so that they would have the things necessary for their own homes when they were married. Pa and Ma went to Whittier to buy dishes. After she unpacked and washed them, a set of snow white dishes sat on the shelf near the door. Pa made a long box that stood on square legs. One side was for flour and the other side for corn meal.

Pa spent many long hours at the sawmill. Ma planted the garden and took care of the livestock. All summer she worked toward making the long winter a comfortable one. She preserved all the food, milked, churned the butter, spun and wove material for clothing, and then hand-sewed all they wore except their shoes. All the energy she had used working for other people could now be used to make a home for her own family.

When the first snow came, they were ready for the isolation it brought. Dried fruit, meat, and vegetables would easily take them through the longest winter. Pa would take his rifle to work sometimes and bring home a squirrel for fresh meat and gravy.

By the last of November, Ma knew that they would be parents by spring. She took special pride in making the baby's clothes. Delicate crocheted and tatted lace trimmed the bonnet and dress. Several pairs of long white stockings were necessary because they were pinned to the baby's diaper and had to be changed every time the diaper was. They had bought soft flannel to make gowns and "belly bands" to wear around the baby's stomach. It was believed that a weakness in the stomach at the navel would cause a rupture if the baby didn't wear the band tightly for six weeks after birth.

Returning in later life to visit her birthplace, Dorie stands near the mud and brick chimney that was part of the fireplace where Ma had cooked all their meals.

In the early spring of 1899, Pa decided to move closer to his job. He rented a small farm near the Cherokee reservation. They loaded their few pieces of furniture on a wagon and moved in time for spring planting. Ma worked along beside him until her time to give birth. I was born May 8, 1899, almost an anniversary gift to them.

The Cherokee women were very curious about Pa and Ma. Many times Ma would look up and see a silent, unsmiling Indian looking in the window or open door. Sometimes, when working outside, she'd catch a fleeting glimpse of them behind the trees. They watched while she boiled and washed the clothing in a big, black wash kettle. The kettle sat on three rocks, over a fire. Ma would bring water from the river to fill the kettle and then build a fire under it.

Pa had driven two posts into the ground and stretched rope between them to hang the clothing out to dry. Some of the articles of clothing fascinated the Indians. They'd touch the white bran-sack sheets and wonder about the use for such a big piece of cloth. Indian women washed their clothes in the river and dried them by draping them over rocks and bushes. It wasn't long before Ma could see clotheslines beside the Indians' cabins. They learned fast.

Ma made friends with some of the women. They taught her how to make Indian bean bread and chestnut dumplings. The bread was made of cornmeal, like cornbread, with cooked dried beans mixed into the dough. Chestnut dumplings were chestnuts covered with cornmeal dough, shaped into a ball, rolled in corn shucks, tied on each end with a strip of shuck, and dropped into boiling water.

The Cherokees had many ways to eat corn. It was roasted, boiled, stewed, ground up, parched, popped, mixed with other vegetables and meat, and baked in many kinds of bread. Over half of the Indian's food was plant food. They favored deer meat and bear meat and caught fish with their bare hands.

They tapped maple sugar trees for sweetening. This, along with wild honey was used for trade. Scuppernong grapes, strawberries, huckleberries, gooseberries, crab apples, and persimmons were staples of their diet in the summer months. Persimmons were used with the corn to make a slightly sweet, cakelike bread.

There was one Cherokee delicacy Ma never tasted—they had a

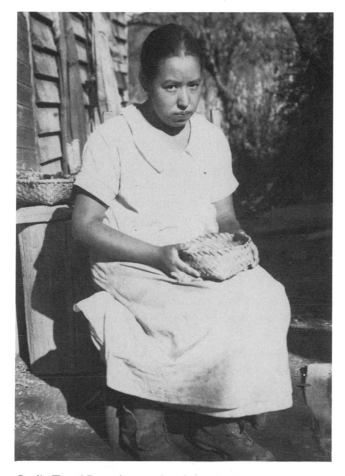

Oevlie Teoni Du-an'e, stepdaughter of Chief Standing Deer
of the Cherokees, is shown weaving a small basket. She was
typical of many of Ma's friends.

fondness for roasted wasp larvae. Finding a new wasp nest just before the young were hatched, they'd take a small stick and remove
the white larvae and roast them over an open fire. It was considered an act of bravery to steal a nest from an angry swarm of wasps.

In the early 1900s it was still common for an Indian man to

have more than one wife. Ma knew several families where there were three wives for one husband. The census taker said he had found one man with six wives. Two seemed enough for most men.

After Ma had won the friendship and respect of the Cherokee women, they began to share their legends with her. One woman told her:

> At one time all living things were in the sky, on the sky rock, and this was before the world was made. All the animals could understand man; and man could understand them. Then man dishonored the privilege and was stricken deaf to the talk of animals and birds. The Great One who was over the sky rock punished man so that he could only understand the talk of his own kind.

Ma loved to hear these stories. She had great admiration for the Indians and said you could learn patience from them. They never hurried with anything. They knew it took time for the giant white oak to grow from a tiny acorn. There was nothing man could do to rush the growth of the seed planted in the ground. Time meant nothing to them. Man must wait for some things to happen. Worry and work could only accomplish so much, the rest was left to the Great One in the sky.

Sometimes we unknowingly broke one of their taboos. The Cherokees never addressed another person directly. To do so was considered rudeness, which the Indian abhorred. This custom indicated reverence for another person's spirit. The spirits of humans and animals were holy to them. They always apologized to an animal they shot and wished its spirit a safe journey to where it was going.

I didn't get to be the baby for long. My sister, Lola, was born October 2, 1900. My only brother, Luther Allen, was born April 8, 1902. The last child, Lydia, was born December 7, 1903. Ma always had a difficult time having her babies. A doctor was never in attendance at the births because there wasn't one in the mountains. Usually Ma's sisters or a midwife from the township delivered the babies. An Indian midwife delivered Luther. Pa gave her a pumpkin for payment. The Indians were fine herb doctors and kind, sympathetic midwives.

From the beginning, Ma had been sick with her last baby. When her time came, Pa bundled Lola, Luther, and me up and took us through the snow to Cousin Martha Carver's house about a mile up the Oconaluftee River. We didn't know Ma was going to have a baby. Pa told us she was sick and couldn't take care of us for a few days.

Aunt Etta Maples came to help with the delivery, and she later told us about the birth. The baby was turned wrong—breech birth, I think. The labor was long and painful. Although the men were usually sent out of the house when children were born, Pa was afraid to leave Ma this time. He felt all along that she would have trouble. He held her in his arms when the pain twisted her body. Tears ran down his face and fell upon hers. In her agony, she thought his tears were rain drops and kept asking why it was raining in the house.

After Lydia was born, Ma lay feverish and sick for many days. She had no milk for the baby. The fever had dried it up. Lydia was starving. Pa went in search of a "wet nurse" for her. Mountain women would sometimes feed someone else's baby when the mother couldn't give milk. He couldn't find a nursing mother and Lydia grew hungrier and weaker. Ma couldn't get out of bed and her mind still confused fact and fantasy. She didn't seem aware of the life and death struggle Pa and the baby faced.

Pa tried to feed Lydia cow's milk and sugar warmed in a china cup set in the coals of the fireplace. He couldn't take her anywhere for medical help. She would have died from exposure in the below-zero weather. The nearest doctor was many miles down the mountain. I can still see Pa sitting by the fireplace holding the tiny white bundle and trying to put drops of milk into the little mouth. He'd cry until the flannel was wet with his tears. He gazed at the small angel face as if he knew he'd have to look at her enough now to last a lifetime. Her kittenlike cry would wake us at night. We knew Pa was still up, rocking her gently by the warmth of the fire.

Lydia died January 1, 1904. Ma's sisters dressed her in a little gown and bonnet Ma had made before she was born. Neighbors came and made the tiny, pine coffin. They lined the inside of it with white flannel and draped black flannel on the outside. Friends and relatives dug the grave in the frozen ground and stood beside us when we gave Lydia back to God. She was buried just outside the Qualla Reservation. Later when Pa and Ma had enough money, they bought a small tombstone for her grave.

Sadness filled our lives for the rest of that winter. Ma wasn't well, and Pa's spirit was broken. We were separated from everyone. Pa couldn't go to work when the snow was so deep. We had our usual share of colds and croup. Ma, frail and unsmiling, used mountain remedies to treat our illnesses. She covered our chests with onion poultices and grease. If the congestion was bad, she gave us the usual three drops of turpentine or kerosene with sugar water. This always broke up the croup. Ma believed that the cough from a late winter cold would last until the leaves fell from the white oak trees in the spring.

So we waited. Snow came two or three times a week to add inches to the blanket already on the ground. Silence hung over the mountains like a misty fog. Tree limbs snapped under the weight of snow and ice. The sharp, sudden noise echoed from mountain peak to mountain peak. Wind whistled around the corners of the cabin and down the chimney, causing the fire to reach out of the fireplace and fill the room with ashes. Ma kept beans and meat boiling in the kettle.

The days, weeks and months all seemed to run together. Every day was the same. Ma kept us fed. Pa tended the livestock and kept wood for the fire. Lola, Luther and I made up our own games to pass the time away. Sometimes Pa sang a dreadfully sad song. It was called "The Drunkard's Last Drink."

Dorie: Woman of the Mountains

One awful dark and stormy night
I heard and saw an awful sight
Lightening flashed and thunder rolled,
It made me think of my poor soul.
I dashed the drink down and left the place,
And went to seek redeeming grace.

I went home to change my life.
And see about my darling wife.
I found her weeping o'er the bed
Because our infant babe was dead.
I took her by her little white hand.
She was so weak she could not stand.
I laid her down and breathed a prayer
That God would bless and save us there.

I told her not to moan nor weep,
Our little babe was just asleep.
Its little soul had fled away
To dwell with Christ in the endless day.

Tears rolled down his face. Ma kept her sorrow inside. They grieved for Lydia in different ways. We never spoke of her but her memory filled the house. Pa had said as they lowered the coffin into the ground, "She'll be waiting for us on the other side."

Spring finally came. Pa and Ma felt better when they could work outside. We had very little money now. Pa hadn't been able to work because of the weather. Ma's hard work last fall had provided us with enough food to last until the garden came in. We still had dried beans, berries, corn cut off the cob, pumpkin sliced and strung on a string and a little cured ham. Gourds hanging from wall pegs held the seeds for a new planting. Pa hunted squirrels and rabbits for fresh meat. Ma didn't like for him to bring in rabbits. People were dying from something called rabbit fever. "Better to be hungry than dead," Ma said.

It was a matter of pride with Pa and Ma that we have biscuits for breakfast. Cornbread was fine for the two other meals, but to eat cornbread for breakfast indicated poverty or laziness or both. Pa always said that while he was alive, we'd never have to eat cornbread for breakfast. Ice cold milk and butter made the biscuits and cornbread taste like dessert.

I was always anxious for the first of May to come because Ma let us go barefoot after that day. Feet that had grown too big for last year's shoes were set free. Also, in preparation for spring, we were all lined up and given our spring tonic of sulphur and molasses. This was supposed to clean out our systems and get rid of all the winter wastes and diseases.

As soon as the weather was warm enough, Ma took us to the banks of the Oconaluftee River, stripped us, took us one by one into the cold, clear water, and washed us with lye soap. The harshness of the soap and the cold water made our bodies turn rosy red. Our long braids were undone and our hair lathered with the soft, jellylike soap Ma kept in a pottery crock. Luther's golden curls picked up every ray of the sun after the last rinse. Rapunzel's golden hair couldn't have been prettier. Ma and Pa would bathe just before twilight. Ma kept on her white petticoat and Pa wore his short, one-piece summer underwear. They never bathed unclothed.

The Oconaluftee River was sacred to the Cherokees, but Ma thought it was alright if we had our weekly baths in the crystal water. "We won't dirty it much," she said. The Indians called the river Ya'nu-dine hunyi, "Where the bears live." A family of water bears was said to live at the bottom of the river in a deep hole. Another part of the river was called Ya'nu-u'nata wasti'yi, "Where the bears wash." It was a deeper part of the river, where all the animals came to wash and heal their wounds when they had been hurt by hunters. No white person had ever seen this place because evil had blinded us to its existence. The animals knew how to find it, and diving into it meant instant healing. Ma never believed any of these legends and said, "A river is a river!" We called it the Luftee River as most white settlers did.

Ma's friend Nancy George Bradley and her family were expert basket weavers.

Spring was the time to renew old acquaintances with relatives and friends whom we hadn't seen since the first big snow last fall. Ma took us all to visit her Indian friends, all the while cautioning us not to eat anything offered. Their visits to our cabin became more frequent. Ma was afraid they'd steal her babies. Many had never seen babies with blue eyes. Luther had blond hair to go with his bright blue eyes. They rubbed his head and talked among themselves about him.

I didn't like to visit the Indians because they always kept so many dogs. Dogs were everywhere in and around their homes. They were frail, scrubby looking animals—eating only meager scraps from the table and the few small animals they caught. I wondered what would happen if the dogs went mad. One of my nightmares was of Indian dogs on the rampage. More than once, I saw them go into convulsive "fits" caused by worms.

Summers were fun for us. Cousin Martha was my playmate

even though she was three years older than I. Early in the morning, I'd wait for her at the Luftee River. She'd play all day and then cross the river and disappear around the mountain path. She lived on one side of the Luftee and we lived on the other. A tree had fallen across the river, making a natural bridge between us.

Swift, clear water rushed under the log making foamy, white whirlpools around the river rocks. Ma told me never to go near the water without her or Pa. I intended to keep my promise to Ma but I never wanted Martha to leave, so sometimes I'd walk to the Luftee with her and then run back home. One day I was very reluctant to give up my playmate and I started home with her. She went on the log first, holding my hand. When we got to the middle, the fast moving water made me dizzy. The log seemed to be moving downstream. I grabbed her dress, causing us both to lose our balance and fall in.

Neither of us could swim. The cold water filled my nose and mouth, and I went down further. The current made it impossible for us to stand up. It was as if someone was pulling our legs out from under us every time we tried to get up. Somehow, Martha dragged herself and me out of the water, which was fighting to keep us. Crying and shaking with fear, we went back to Ma. Instead of reassurance, she gave me a thrashing with a maple switch. Martha got a tongue-lashing for letting me follow her. Poor Martha. She had nothing to do with me tagging along behind her and she was quick-witted enough to save me. I don't recall ever being in the Luftee River again. Indeed, I felt so afraid of water I never learned to swim.

After my seventh birthday, Pa and Ma began talking about school for me. It was miles to the nearest school and neither of them had the time nor the inclination to walk with me morning and evening. I was too small to go alone. "Times are changing," Pa said, "She'll need an education—a better one than we had."

They decided the best thing for me was to go to school in Waynesville. Pa's mother and stepfather, Queenie and Ruben Mills, lived there. School was in walking distance, and they said I'd be more than welcome to live with them. My grandparents were strangers to me. I didn't want to leave home and live with them.

"Grandpa Ruben will be here Saturday to take you back with him," Ma said. "I'll have to get all your things ready." Ma sewed, washed, and ironed my clothes. We didn't have many clothes to wear. We only had two dresses, and we wore one dress all week. They were straight, simple dresses that came to our ankles. Ma cut out a basic pattern with long sleeves, long skirt, and no collar. We wore muslin slips and pantaloons that came to our knees. Our coats and winter dresses were made from stiff, scratchy wool. Only age softened the fabric—but, by then, we would have outgrown the clothing and had to start all over again with new, stiff, scratchy material.

Each passing day brought the dreaded time nearer. I cried at night, softly so no one would hear me. Every time Pa passed me, he'd smile and gently pat my head.

Early Saturday morning Pa hitched the horses to the wagon and went to meet the train. Grandpa Ruben was coming on a train that was going somewhere south—just making a stop to let him off in Bryson City. We would catch another train that afternoon going back toward Waynesville. I heard Pa and the wagon stop in front of our house. When Grandpa Ruben came through the door, my heart sank. I think I hated him then.

Ma had dinner ready soon after they arrived. Grandpa, Ma, and Pa talked and laughed while they ate. The golden fried chicken would have made my mouth water any other time. Today, everything I put into my mouth tasted like cotton. It wouldn't go down. We had to leave on the three o'clock train, and I was sure I'd never be happy again.

Ma packed my clothes in a box, and Pa put me and the box in the wagon. I sat between him and Grandpa. Ma, Lola, and

Luther stood in the doorway and waved goodbye. My throat was tight and had a lump as big as an apple. I tried to swallow it, but it stuck fast. Pa talked gently to the horses, not saying anything directly to me lest I begin crying. Pa never knew what to do when a woman cried.

The train depot smelled of smoke and oil. The tracks went into infinity, taking me away from everything I knew and loved. I looked both ways, up and down the tracks, wondering where they began and where they ended. Loud, shrill noises came from the black monster approaching. Smoke swept back in a white streak from the smoke stack. It stopped in front of us. Pa took my hand and we boarded a passenger car. Grandpa said I could sit by the window so I could see Pa after he got off. I wanted to wave goodbye to him. The train jerked forward, throwing me into the back of the seat in front of us and then slammed me back again into my own seat. When I could sit up and look out the window, Pa was already left behind. I didn't get to wave goodbye, and I didn't know when I'd see him again.

After the train started, it swayed back and forth, making my head and stomach feel uneasy. Grandpa Ruben didn't say much to me. We were strangers, and there was nothing to talk about. Misery filled my soul. Large tears rolled down my cheeks. On the silent trip to Waynesville, I thought about home and wondered if I'd ever get back.

The train frightened me and made me remember dreams I'd had since I was four years old. Even though I'd never seen a train, I'd dream about a sleek, shiny, black machine running along tracks, pulling deep boxes filled with an equally black, shiny substance in chunks. When I tried to describe it to Ma, she'd laugh and say, "Dorie, you've never seen a train, and there is no such cars like that." Many years later, I saw the train in my dreams and it was pulling cars piled high with coal.

School was terrifying. It was a one-room building full of strange children of assorted sizes. The small children sat up front near the teacher's desk, while the large, menacing boys and girls sat in the back. Grandpa Ruben took my hand and led me up the front steps to meet the teacher. She told me to sit beside a small blonde girl who sat alone in a desk made to be shared by two children. The moment Grandpa went out of the door, I started to cry. The girl beside me patted my hand and tried to get me to look at her book, but great sobs shook my body.

Every day was the same. I was brave until I was left at school. For three weeks I did nothing but cry. Finally, the teacher couldn't stand it anymore. She told Grandpa I was too young to be taken away from my family and I was making her job very difficult. Three weeks of school had taught me nothing. Not one A, B, or C had found its way into my brain. My ignorance was still intact, but I didn't care. I was going home. That was all that mattered.

Grandpa and I got back on the train going toward Ocona–luftee. I knew Ma and Pa would be disappointed in me. They were surprised when we walked into the house. Disapproval was evident in Ma's face. "Do you want to be ignorant all your life?," Ma asked. Pa didn't say so, but he was glad to have me home. He looked at me and smiled a slow, happy smile. He understood why I had come home. I'd never have Ma's strength or nerve. She was made of steel and I was made of clay.

I walked around the room, touching every piece of furniture, every familiar thing. I ran out the door and around the cabin. Everything was the same, just as I had dreamed about it every night. Grandpa Ruben would go home tomorrow and everything would be the same again—like it was before I went away.

Pa and Grandpa talked far into the night. They talked about cotton mills out beyond the mountains. Grandpa said a man could earn more money than he could use by working in the mills. "Why don't you and Lila come, too?" he asked. "I'm doing alright here 'til the job runs out," Pa said. "If times get hard, we might join you. Spartanburg's a long way to move unless you mean to stay."

I was happy to be home. Cousin Martha thought I was still in Waynesville so I had to play with Lola and Luther. Pa said he'd tell her to come see me when he went her way. Ma said she'd teach me to read and write in the winter when we were snowed in.

"There's more to school than reading and writing, Dorie," she'd say. "Out beyond these mountains another world exists. You may have to live out there where everything is different and we can't have you ignorant."

Ma was so capable. She hadn't been to school much, but she was schooled in the art of mountain living. If she couldn't educate me with books, she was determined to teach me how to make a living. An expert in so many crafts, I only had to mention one and she was ready to show me how it was done.

Willow and white oak splits made beautiful and useful baskets. Gourds were grown and cured to be used as dippers in the water buckets or as handy wall containers for seeds. We had a row of broom corn in every garden. Ma made our sweeping and dusting brooms from this. Our scrubbing broom was made from a hickory limb about the size of a person's arm. Carefully, the limb was hewn back until the strips were about three inches from the other end. When the limb was a good size for a broom handle, all the strips were gathered at the other end and tied over the uncut part. The stiff strips were cut evenly across. With this broom and lye soap, almost any floor would be bleached as white as chalk.

So many plants and flowers could be used for sickness. Slowly, I learned what was good for the afflictions of man. We gathered cockleburrs to be boiled into a cough syrup for winter colds. Tansy was a fern-like plant used as tea for upset stomachs and headaches. Boneset and catnip were brewed into tea for fretful babies and nervous disorders. Sassafras was a good blood builder. Spignet root was kidney medicine. Crushed ragweed was rubbed on skin blistery from poison ivy and oak. Tobacco juice and/or mud stopped the pain and itch from insects' stings and bites. The pinpoint-sized red devil—the chigger—was subdued by thick, brown tobacco juice, too. Kerosene was applied to cuts, bruises, and puncture wounds. Summer boils and risings were brought to a head by a poultice of cornmeal or oatmeal.

Nobody went to the doctor for anything except appendicitis or amputations. No self-respecting woman would allow a doctor to be present when her child was born. It was "unseemly" for a man to see a woman in so degrading a position. Everything we needed was all around us. We had to have the intelligence and strength to make it work for us.

Ma was an expert at spinning, weaving, and dying material for our clothing. Early ancestors had brought flax seed from Scotland and Ireland when they came to America. Flax grew around the cabin or in the garden. The flowers, which we were not allowed to pick, could range in color from deep blue to very pale blue.

After the seeds had formed and were ready to harvest, we pulled up the whole plant by the roots.. If the crops were abundant, the seeds were mixed with the cow's food. Some of the seeds were crushed and drained to get a light oil used as medicine. The best ones were saved for planting and for wedding gifts to the young people starting their own homes.

The stalks were spread out on the ground where rain and dew would cause the outer skin to rot, separating the fibers from the woody portions outside. The long, straight fibers were twisted together to make thread, which was wound on spindles and later woven into material for dresses, underwear, and linens for the house. It became the "linsey" part of linsey-woolsey —so well known from the Western frontier days.

In the late spring or early summer, Pa, Uncle Julius and Uncle Aden sheared the sheep. They had to wait until the weather was warm because the fleece is cut close to the skin, leaving the sheep almost bare. If they sheared the sheep before Dogwood Winter (usually in May), it was likely some of the sheep would die from exposure. Wool from the shoulders of the sheep is better than that taken from other parts. Ma used the shoulder wool for dresses. The stiffer wool made heavy coats that were rainproof.

Ma would card the wool—straightening out the curly-kinky hair so that it could be spun into thread. A small loom stood by the corner window for the needed sunlight. Ma would weave the yarn into cloth. In the mountains, if somebody tells you that you are "all wool and a yard wide," take it as a sincere compliment. It means you are real, genuine, and honest.

The wool never lost the odor of sheep. When Pa came in after being in the rain, his coat had the faint, lingering odor of sheep. We got used to the aroma of lye soap and wet wool. In the terrible days of winter, we were thankful for enough clothing to keep us warm.

Although Ma could make pretty colors of dye for the thread, we wore dull, drab colors of black, gray, brown, or dark blue. That way, our dresses didn't show dirt before the end of the week, when it was time to change dresses.

Mountain women had strange notions about the colors they wore. Wedding dresses were chosen with great care, if they could afford one at all. Their future as a wife could depend on the right color choice.

Marry in white. . . . you'll surely fight
Marry in red. . . . . . you'll wish yourself dead
Marry in green. . . . you'll be ashamed to be seen
Marry in brown. . . you'll live in a town
Marry in blue. . . . . you'll always be true
Marry in black. . . . you'll wish yourself back
Marry in yellow . . . you've got the right fellow

Ma had a friend who made a white blouse and a green skirt for her wedding. The older women scolded her until she cried. The skirt was died a musty gray before she wore it again.

Most everything we needed for colored dye could be found around the cabin or up on the mountains surrounding us. "The Lord provides," Ma always said. Here is what she used:

Dorie: Woman of the Mountains

Plant	Part to Use	Color
Onion	Skins	Yellow-orange
Hickory	Bark	Yellow
Apple	Twigs	Yellow
Black-eyed Susan	Plant above ground	Yellow
Black Oak	Bark	Yellow
Blackberries	Berries	Pink
Carrot	Tops	Lime-green
Dahlia	Red flowers	Orange-gold
Dandelion	Flowers	Yellow
Dandelion	Plant	Lime-green
Grapes	Fruits	Lavender
Iris	Purple flowers	Light-blue
Mustard	Plant	Light-green
Partridge Pea	Flowers	Rust
Black Walnut	Outer skin of nut	Dark-brown

All the light, bright colors were used to dye thread for crocheting doilies, embroidery, and tatting lace for pretty things for the house.

Although she was very good at dying and weaving, Ma was sad about two things. No matter how many times she tried, she couldn't make a red dye. The nearest color was orange or rust. The other thing that made her sad was that wool always smelled like the sheep that had worn it first.

Late in the summer, a letter came to Pa from his mother. She and Grandpa Ruben were in Spartanburg, South Carolina, working in a cotton mill. Their children, Polly and Tom, were with them. New cotton mills were opening in Georgia and South Carolina, and pay was good. Many mountaineers were going out to the lowlands in search of a better life. In the fall of 1906, Pa and Ma decided to go to Spartanburg because Pa's job had run out and they would have to move somewhere to find another one.

Ma packed all our dried fruit, vegetables, and cured pork into baskets. All our clothing and bedding were packed in barrels. One barrel held the dishes, pots, and pans. Our only furniture was a table, four chairs, two double beds, and a feather bed. The mattresses on the beds were emptied of their straw. We would refill them again at our new home. A friend of Pa's put all the boxes on his wagon and took us to the railroad station in Bryson City.

I was going to enjoy this train ride. All my family was with me this time. Lola and I sat together on a seat, while Luther sat between Ma and Pa. "Hold on tight when the train starts or you'll get hurt," I warned. I felt very pleased with myself because I had been on a train before and Lola and Luther hadn't.

Trees rushed by the window. Soon the land was getting flat and the mountains were left behind. I had to turn around and look over my shoulder to see the hazy, blue mountains. Big, white, cottony thunderhead clouds were all I could see that reminded me of the little cabin left behind. Grandpa Ruben and Tom met us at the depot. We were going to stay with them while Pa went to the mills. They left our barrels and furniture on the wagon because Grandpa said Pa was sure to have a job and a house in a day or two.

Pa easily found work and a house that belonged to the company. We would have to pay rent to them. The house was much better than the cabin in the mountains. A shiny, black cookstove stood in the kitchen and a water pump at the back door. Our water had always come from a mountain stream or spring. How fascinating that water gushed from a little black pump with a handle that went up and down! Ma had never had a cookstove before. All our food had been prepared at a fireplace, with Ma stooping over to stir and turn the pots. Now she could stand tall and cook. All the pots and pans were waist-high and easy to get to.

Life was easier for us. We children liked our new home. For one thing, there were other children to play with and new and wonderful things to discover. But, still, Ma and Pa were not happy. Pa didn't like being cooped up in the mills. His free, mountain spirit was cramped. He'd worked out in the open air all his life. The linty, noisy mills were more than he could bear. "Some of the foremen call us lint-heads," he said. "I don't like being called names."

Dorie, Luther Allen, and Lola Woodruff (*left to right*) pose in better clothing bought while Pa worked in Spartanburg, South Carolina. The little girls always had necklaces.

There wasn't any snow that winter. Ma thought it would be nice to have some snow for Christmas, but none came. Winter rains kept the yards and roads covered with puddles. Everything was caked with mud. Ma said it looked like the Good Lord would send us just a little snow to hide the "ugly places" for a while.

Until we moved here, we'd never celebrated Christmas. The day came and went like any other day. Our new friends talked about hanging up their stockings and what they wanted Santa Claus to bring them. Lola, Luther, and I begged Ma to let us hang up our stockings to see what we'd get. "Alright," she said, "but don't expect much. Christmas is a day for quiet thoughts, and, if giving is done, it's good deeds and good will that should be given away—not frills and playthings."

Christmas morning dawned a rainy, gray day. We waited until Pa got the fire going before we got up. I was almost afraid to look in my stocking—afraid it would be empty. All three of our stockings were lumpy and stretched longer. Something was in there! I put my hand into mine and out came a striped candy cane. Next came a big red apple and, finally, a bright orange ball.

"What is this, Ma?"

"An orange," she said. "Why do you suppose they're called oranges?"

"Because they're orange colored," we said. "What do we do with them, Ma?"

"Silly gooses, you eat them."

She laughed as she showed us how to eat the oranges. She said we could make a hole in the end and suck out the juice, or we could take the skin off and the fruit would come apart. We could eat each little piece and make it last longer. Ma took a knife and gently cut into the skin. We peeled it away, and there was the juiciest, most delicious thing I'd ever tasted. The candy and the apple were put away for later. It didn't matter that Santa Claus had not brought playthings. We didn't know about Santa Claus, and I guess he didn't know about us. The day had been exciting and happy. Never again could I eat an orange without remembering my first one, nestling in the toe of my Christmas stocking.

Soon after Christmas, Luther got sick. He had a high fever and a terrible cough. Ma knew he had pneumonia. Pa said the company doctor would come by to see him. The doctor agreed with Ma's diagnosis; Luther had a bad case of pneumonia. "Keep a cold cloth on his head to keep down the fever and give him quinine three times a day," he said.

Ma was enraged. Quinine and a cold cloth on his head wouldn't be any help curing the disease ravaging his lungs. She went to the kitchen and sliced a dozen onions into a greasy pan. When the onions were wilted and greasy, she covered Luther's chest with them and wrapped him with quilts. In a little while he started coughing, and in the night his fever broke.

Ma didn't have much good to say about doctors and their medicine. Mountain know-how would beat lowland medicine anytime. The Good Book says there are herbs on earth to cure all the diseases of humanity. Without quinine and iodine, the "educated" doctor couldn't practice his trade.

Luther was frail and weak for a long time. "He's going to die unless we get him back to God's Country where the air is pure and the water's good," Ma said.

Lonely and homesick, they longed to return to the mountains. Ma had received a letter from her mother asking us to come to Tennessee and help them farm. Ma's mother, Granny Jane, had married John Watson, one of Oldham's Creek's early settlers. He had orchards and a farm of many acres, reaching from the Glades to Boogertown.

For reasons I never knew, Oldham's Creek was also called Boogertown. Both names were used interchangeably in the same conversation. The only time Oldham's Creek was always used was in connection with the Baptist Church. I've never heard it called Boogertown Baptist Church.

"The Lord surely answers prayers," Ma said. "When can we get away from here?" Pa said his paycheck wouldn't buy tickets for us all the way to Sevierville and pay the freight cost for the furniture. Ma took all our dried fruit, vegetables, and cured pork and sold them for enough money to send our belongings to Sevierville, and with Pa's money it was enough to get tickets for us as far as Smokemont.

Granny and Grandpa Mills were going to stay and work in the mills. Several of the families were leaving when we did—in time to get a garden planted and find summer work. Many of the mountaineers who thought the cotton mills were the pot of gold at the end of the rainbow soon found they didn't like what was in the pot. The air was bad, the water tasted funny and they didn't like being subjected to the whims of the overseers. The things they valued most, freedom and independence, were gone.

Ma didn't have much to put into the barrels this time. All the food was gone. One barrel held our clothing and the household linens, and one barrel held the pots and pans. When we got off the train in Smokemont, our furniture would go on to Sevierville, where Pa would pick it up later for the trip to Boogertown.

"Why do you call it Boogertown, Pa? It sounds like it's haunted," I asked. Pa laughed. "I reckon it's because so many ugly people live there. I'll fit right in, but you'll pretty up the place some."

A long time before I could see the mountains, the thunderheads rose to greet us. The sky was a blue as a robin's egg. About noon, I could see the faint, pale purple outline of the Smokies. Nothing ever looked so beautiful.

"Times will be hard," Pa said. "Well, if we starve to death, we'll be in a place worth dying for," Ma said.

Uncle Aden Carver met us at the depot. He said we'd grown a foot since we'd been gone, but Luther looked a "mite peaked." Uncle Aden was a colorful and respected mountaineer. He had many talents like Ma. He was a farmer, a stonecutter, a carpenter, and a miller.

"Don't hear much from our folks since they moved to the Tennessee side," he said. "Your Ma (Granny Jane) hasn't been back since she married John Watson. Looks like I'm going to be the only Carver left in North Carolina."

Most of Ma's sisters and aunts had married and moved to Tennessee. Aunt Etta married Houston Ball and lived on Webb's Creek, Aunt Sally had married John Bright and lived on Webb's Creek, Aunt Isabel married John Barnes and lived in Greenbrier, Aunt Cora married Harrison Ogle and lived on the lower

Uncle Aden Carver's home represented a place where "better times" existed for Dorie's family.

end of Middle Creek. Of course, Ma's youngest and favorite sister, Aunt Rintha married David Coin Watson and lived across the road from Granny Jane and John Watson.

Uncle Aden still lived on the banks of the Oconaluftee, and Uncle Julius lived in the next cabin around the bend. Pa and Ma walked silently to the banks of the Luftee and gazed into the clear water. It had been a long time since they'd seen anything as beautiful as a speckled trout swimming lazily along the bottom of the river. "Just leave them be," Uncle Aden said to us. "They're glad to be home. Come on in the house and we'll see what's to eat."

The next day Ma wrote Uncle Dave Watson to see if he could bring enough horses for us to ride to Boogertown. The trails were narrow and rough. If we brought a wagon, we'd have to travel further and go over the mountain at Newfound Gap. The shortest distance could be traveled by horseback or on foot. If it hadn't been for us children, Ma and Pa would have walked across the mountain. It was done almost every day. About a week later, Uncle Dave came. He was riding a horse, and another one was hitched to the saddle.

Just as the sun peeked over the mountain the next morning, we started on our way to Tennessee. A cool fog hung low over the ground. Almost like a living thing, it moved around us. A dense patch would suddenly disappear only to engulf us again a few steps further on. We had to wear coats until the sun was fully up and every trace of the fog was gone. Lola and I rode one horse. Ma sometimes rode with Luther. Mostly, she walked and admired the spring wildflowers.

Miniature, pale green leaves gently fluttered in the cool, brisk breeze. From up on the horse, I could reach out and pull them from the low branches hanging over the trail. Along the side of the path, tiny violets looked up at us and smiled. We were all happy to be home again.

At noon we stopped for lunch. Cold biscuits and ham, boiled eggs, and baked sweet potatoes made a delicious meal. Uncle Dave went a little distance off the trail, stooped down, and pulled up something that looked like new onions or lily sprouts.

"Ramps are up," he said. "Nothing like 'em to make everything taste better!"

"What are ramps, Ma?"

"They're like onions, only more so," she laughed.

Uncle Dave shared his ramps with Pa and Ma, but I wouldn't eat them. The smell was so strong that it burned my nose and made my eyes water. Luther offered the horses a handful. They sneezed and shook their heads.

The day dragged on. My backside was beginning to get sore, when it had any feeling at all. We could walk a while if we could keep up with the adults. "Can't have the dark catch us here. I didn't bring my rifle and there are panthers about," Uncle Dave told us.

Late in the evening, Uncle Dave said we were in the Glades and it wouldn't be long now. The hills looked different than any I'd ever seen before. They were smooth and round on the

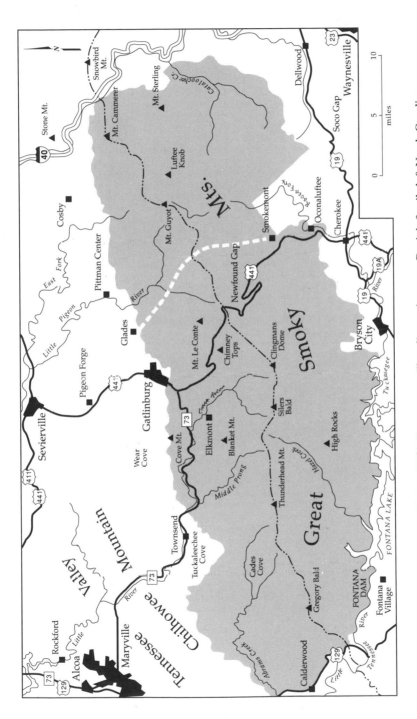

Map 2. From Smokemont to the Glades, 1907. The cotton mills a disappointment, Dorie's family left North Carolina, riding horses over the mountains, to join other family who were farming in Boogertown, Tennessee.

top as if the Creator had shaped them with His own hands. The Glades was a flat place at the base of several rounded hills. We stopped at the Glades Store. Pa went in and bought three sticks of penny candy for Luther, Lola, and me.

Uncle Dave announced that Old Sol (the sun) goes to bed early around here. Sure enough, Old Sol slipped behind a round mountain. Almost as if to let us know he was still there, golden sun streaks reached like outstretched fingers into the clouds. We were going on a trail between two hills when I saw the back of a cabin near the edge of a hollow.

That's home, we were told, and it sure looked good to us weary travelers. We knew we could stretch our legs and get something warm to eat. Supper was probably waiting for us. I could hardly wait. I wanted to eat and meet my cousins, but, most of all, I wanted off that horse. My whole body ached and my legs didn't want to hold me up.

We had really crossed the high, blue mountain, which had become a deep purple in the fading sunlight. The mountain no longer held my interest. A smiling woman in the door of the cabin was beckoning us to come into the soft, yellow light of home.

For the first time, I met Ma's sister and her children. Some of the girls were my age. The introductions and greetings were short so we could sit down at the table for our first meal in Tennessee. Aunt Rintha had fixed a good supper for us, but I was so tired everything tasted the same.

"Too tired to eat?" she asked. "These children need to be put to bed. I wouldn't have known Dorie. She was a tiny baby when I saw her . . . a pretty one, too. She looks like her Pa with that sharp chin and high cheekbones. Lola's more like you and me, Lilah. She could be one of mine. Where did Luther get all that blond hair?"

Cousin Dicie, Aunt Rintha's oldest daughter, put pallets on the floor for us. When I went to sleep, Ma and Aunt Rintha were catching up on all the family news while Pa and Uncle Dave talked about farming.

The smell of sausage and eggs woke us the next morning. Dicie was helping her Ma with breakfast. My backside was sore from riding the horse all day. When I tried to stand up, every muscle in my body ached. What I didn't eat last night I made up for this morning. My insides felt hollow and hungry.

After breakfast, Dicie took Lola and me outside for our first real look at our new home. Rolling, rounded hills completely surrounded us. I had to look straight up to see the sky. Over to our right, Granny Jane's house sat at the edge of a beautiful orchard. Our house was a one-room cabin on a hill across the orchard. Between us, trees covered with white and pink flowers filled the hollow. Across the road from Granny's, a sparkling creek ran through the meadow. A huge barn stood ready for us to explore. This seemed like a very special place, almost as if we were the only people in the world and this land our Eden.

II

1907–1912

Ma and Pa started work on the cabin so we'd have a place of our own. They scrubbed, mended, and filled cracks between the logs. The rock and mud fireplace had to be rebuilt. Pa built a lean-to for a kitchen. Ma papered the inside with newspaper brought back from Spartanburg. We thought it was the cleanest, prettiest house in the world. The front door faced the orchard. Two lop-sided windows on each side of the door sparkled from their vinegar-and-water scrubbing.

I was warned to watch out for Uncle Jimmy Maples' big tom turkey, which he was fattening up to sell. He played with the turkey, teased it, and taunted it until it knew every mean trick. All of us girls were afraid of him.

Ma sent me across the orchard to get a bucket of water out of Granny Jane's well. I got the water and was walking along, humming to myself, when something hit me in the back. I landed face down in the dirt and the water bucket went flying through the air. The turkey had sneaked up behind me, taken a running go, hit me with his big, dirty feet, and flogged me with his wings. In a rage, I picked up the bucket and bashed him across the back again and again. I didn't hurt him. He waddled off as if nothing had happened. I dusted myself off and went to get another bucket of water.

We always had to watch for him. His favorite hiding place was a drainage ditch in the middle of the orchard. From there, he could plan his ambush and never be seen. I was glad when he was sold to the peddler. It didn't matter to me if he was somebody's Sunday dinner.

Pa and Uncle Dave went to Sevierville to get our furniture at the train depot. It had been there almost three weeks since it

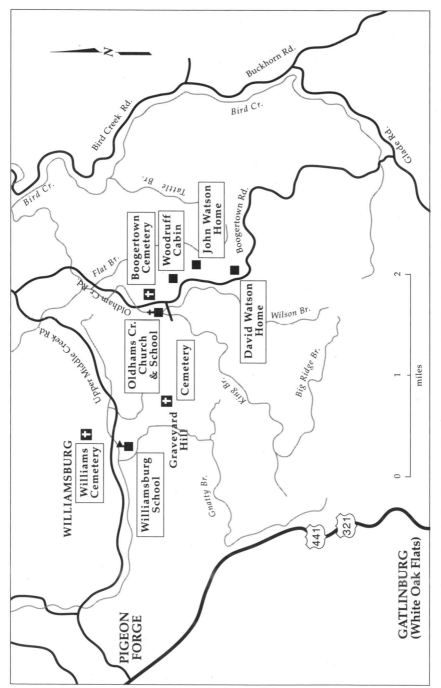

Map 3. Sevier County. Dorie's family farmed in Boogertown until 1912, when a dry spell ruined their luck with the crops.

was brought from Spartanburg. Pa bought a shiny, black "step-stove" for Ma's new kitchen. Granny Jane fed us from her pantry, since we had no food stored away. We'd been living off other people since Ma sold our food to buy tickets back to the mountains. The garden would be in soon and we could be self-sufficient again. Pa said he didn't like eating off other people, benefiting from somebody else's hard work.

We children did our share of the farming, but we had plenty of time to play. The days were long and warm. The woods called us to come, and our Indian blood answered. Cousin Richard, Cousin Arthur, and Uncle Noah would cut big grape vines, and we'd swing like monkeys from one side of the hollow to the other. We built playhouses in the side of the hills and covered the dirt floors with soft, green moss. Flat slate rocks made fine furniture, and acorn caps were china fit for a queen. Our fashionable hats were made from tulip poplar leaves. Little twigs were used like straight pins to hold them together. Reedlike grass along the creek became beautiful jewelry when we braided it and decorated it with dandelion and pink sorrell. Stone bruises covered our feet; our legs and arms were scratched from climbing and rolling down the hillside. Ma said we acted worse than any wild Indian she'd ever seen.

Indians had claimed this place as their own a long time ago. Arrowheads of many sizes and colors could be found on the creek bottom among the rocks. Sometimes Pa or Uncle Dave would find them when they plowed up a new field. I wondered whether the arrowheads had washed down the streams from a distant place or whether the Indians had made them right where I stood. Some arrowheads were black, some gray, and some pink-orange. Along the edges of the water, freshwater oysters and periwinkles clung to the rocks. Probably a little Indian had played here and wished that she, too, would remain a child and never have to leave.

On Sundays we had to become civilized again. Our sore feet were pushed into shoes, our bodies cleansed by the usual Saturday night bath, and we wore our best clothes, taken down

Ma and Pa's household goods were brought from Spartanburg, South Carolina, to Sevierville, Tennessee, on this train, "Old Slow and Easy." They had only enough money to send their belongings on the train, so they walked across the mountain.

from the nails on the walls, so we would appear as clean, well-bred children in church. We walked to the church and sang as we went.

Sunday School was fun. The teacher gave us a small card with a picture and a Bible verse to be memorized for the next Sunday. The pictures were beautiful. Sometimes we'd get Moses with the Ten Commandments, Moses parting the sea, Moses as a baby in the basket, or one of many different pictures of Jesus. My favorite card was one of Jesus standing outside a door, knocking to get in. The verse said: "Behold, I stand at the door, and knock: if any man hear my voice, and open the door, I will come in to him, and will sup with him, and he with me." (Revelation 3:20.)

Dorie: Woman of the Mountains

Preachers who came to Oldham's Creek believed in preaching the wrath of God. Sometimes they'd get caught up in a sermon, raising their voices and shouting. They'd pace back and forth, pointing their fingers at the sinners in the church. When I thought of all the small sins I'd committed during the week, I could see the black smoke of hell boiling up behind them and smell the brimstone seeping up between the cracks in the floor. God was seldom presented as a God of love. " 'Vengeance is mine,' saith the Lord," echoed from the ceiling and pierced the souls of the listeners. My Sunday School cards said "God is love," while the preacher said "Fear the Lord." I felt more fear of the Lord then than love.

Ma always said they were "trunk Baptists." I laughed because I could imagine us all going to church in a trunk. She explained they were called trunk Baptists because she kept their letter of membership in the big trunk beside her bed. They had been members of the Smokemont Baptist Church, but since they moved they hadn't belonged to any church. I almost wished she hadn't explained, because Baptists in a trunk was funnier to think about.

School started the last of August. The term would run until harvest time when we were all needed at home to work. The church building was also used for the school. It sat in a flat place where the road went in three directions. A stream ran in front of the building. People who joined the church were baptized in the water during the warm days. Nobody ever tested their faith by being baptized in the winter time. "Thou shalt not tempt the Lord thy God," Pa said. "Pneumonia's not easy to cure."

Children walked two or more miles to school in the morning and back home again in the afternoon. Tardiness was not permitted. If we were going to play along the way, we had to leave home earlier. Some of the children had to get up as early as five o'clock to do their chores and get to school on time. All six grades were together in one room.

Our teacher, Horace Williams, was the best we'd ever had.

He knew and understood shy mountain children. It didn't matter to him that we smelled of lye soap, wore the same dress all week, and had bare, dusty feet. He lifted the little ones on his lap and taught them poetry and songs. "You can be as smart as anybody and go as far as anybody, if you try," he told us.

I hadn't been to school since my shameful failure in Waynesville. Pa and Ma had taught me to read and write, so I started in the second McGuffey reader and speller. Learning was going to be fun, but playing at recess and walking to and from school with my cousins was going to be even more fun.

We had a special song all the grades sang together. It was an easy way to learn geography and was lots of fun.

> Oh, what did Tenna-see, boys, what did Tenna-see?
> (Tennessee)
> I ask you men, as a personal friend,
> What did Tenna-see?
> She saw what Arkin-saw, boys, she saw what Arkin-saw. (Arkansas)
> I'll tell you then, as a personal friend,
> She saw what Arkin-saw.
> Where has Ora-gone, boys? (Oregon)
> She's taking Okla-home, boys. (Oklahoma)
> How did Wiscon-sin, boys? (Wisconsin)
> She stole a New-brass-key, boys. (Nebraska)
> What did Dela-ware, boys? (Delaware)
> She wore a New Jersey, boys. (New Jersey)
> Where did Ida-hoe, boys (Idaho)
> She hoed in Merry-land, boys. (Maryland)
> What did Io-weigh, boys? (Iowa)
> She weighed a Washing-ton, boys. (Washington)
> What did Missy-sip, boys? (Mississippi)
> She sipped her Mini-soda, boys. (Minnesota)
> What did Connie-cut, boys? (Connecticut)
> She cut her shaggy Mane, boys. (Maine)
> What did Ohi-owe, boys? (Ohio)
> She owed her Taxes, boys. (Texas)
> How did Flora-die, boys? (Florida)
> She died of Misery, boys. (Missouri)

On our walk home after school, we girls sang the question and the boys sang the answer. By the time we got within sight of the farm, we'd named all the states.

The two-mile walk was filled with adventure. About a mile from home, we'd pause at Mr. Watson's and watch his peacock. I'd never seen a bird so very beautiful. If we came near the fence, he'd spread his colorful, fanlike tail feathers and show off for us. The little pea hen wasn't pretty at all. I felt sorry for her because her husband got to wear all the beautiful feathers and prance around. She was a small, brown, timid thing. It all seemed turned around. Girls were supposed to be fancier than boys.

Further on down the road, we'd all huddle together and walk on the other side of the road—away from Andy Marshall's dog. He was a big, mean dog with a big bark. He didn't come out of the yard, but he acted so mean we were afraid. Richard, Noah, and Arthur said they weren't afraid of him, but they stayed as far away as we did.

The Marshalls seemed wealthy to me. Ma and I had visited with them in the summer. They had an organ in a room built especially for it. Mrs. Marshall let me stand in the doorway and look at it, but I couldn't touch it. It was beautiful. I had no idea what kind of sound it would make. Other than Ma's banjo, a guitar, a fiddle, and a Jew's harp, I'd never heard any kind of musical instrument. I wanted Mrs. Marshall to play it for me, but she and Ma were busy talking.

Chestnut trees grew along the road. Filling our hands and pockets with the nuts, we'd go into Lige Wilson's little store to trade. The store was on the right side of the road to school, in one of the few flat places between the hills. We traded chestnuts for slates and pencils, and sometimes we'd get candy to go with our lunch. Lunch was always biscuits and pork, fruit or baked sweet potatoes, and an occasional piece of stack cake.

Fridays were my favorite days. Spelling bees were held every Friday afternoon. The smaller children didn't last long in the contest. Then, one by one, the older boys and girls missed words and sat down. Dicie and I went down in the last round, or, more often, one of us won. We'd study all week so our chances would be good.

All my books were exciting. People and places different from our own small world filled every page. Abraham Lincoln could have been a part of the world where we still lived. He, too, read by oil lamp or candle light. His clothes were rough and home-made like ours, and he lived in a one-room log cabin. It didn't seem possible that he had been born in 1809, a hundred years ago. Were we that far behind the rest of the world? We were living like Mr. Lincoln now. We could understand his world, but the other world—of kings and queens, or princes and prin-cesses, wealth and fame—were only in fairy stories. How could two different worlds exist on so small a place as the earth?

Out beyond the mountains lay a fantasy world: snowy white beaches covered with seashells, foamy ocean water keeping time with the moon, railroad cars with soft beds in private rooms, fancy hats and dresses bought in a store, silver, gold, crystal and china on white linen tablecloths, chairs that were cushioned and soft to sit on, and buildings that held enough books to read in a lifetime. Poets and writers wrote about these things, so they must be true. Out beyond the rounded hills of Boogertown, life was different and hard to understand. Were we backward and poor, or were we more blessed because we were isolated and unaware of the worldly progress? Questions filled my head. The answers were hard to find.

Fall was coming and we knew our school days were few. In September, nature begins to paint the mountains in vivid col-ors. Dogwood trees put on their red dress first. Soon they were joined by yellow poplar, scarlet and yellow maples, and the oak in shades of brown. Goldenrod, blue and white fall asters, Queen Anne's lace, and lacy, purple flowers grew along the road.

On both sides of the road, field after field had shocks of corn and orange pumpkins. The scent of drying tobacco came from the barns. Tobacco meant winter clothing and food for most people. Neighbors helped each other when it was time to grade and "hand-off" the tobacco. It would be taken to Knoxville to be sold at giant warehouses. Pa always kept some to make a twist for chewing and some to chop and age for his pipe.

The morning breeze already turned our noses red and made toes on bare feet sting. A poem in my second reader always described fall best for me.

"Come little leaves," said the wind one day,
"Come o'er the meadow with me and play;
Put on your dresses of red and gold,
For summer is gone, and the days grow cold."

Soon as the leaves heard the wind's loud call,
Down they came fluttering, one and all;
Over the brown fields they danced and flew,
Singing the soft little songs they knew.

Dancing and whirling, the little leaves went,
Winter had called them, and they were content;
Soon, fast asleep in their earthly beds,
The Snow laid a coverlet over their heads.

Hickory nuts and black walnuts fell soon after the leaves. Ma sent Lola, Luther, and me out to pick up as many as we could. Ma sometimes went with us and filled her long apron with them. Hickory nuts shed their outside covering before we picked them up, but the walnuts still kept their green, rough skin. We stored them in a dry place until their skin turned brown. The green walnuts oozed a juice that stained your hands yellow-brown and was impossible to wash off.

My hands had stains all fall. I kept them in my lap as much as possible at school. Eventually, the dye faded, and, by then, it was time to remove the brown outer skin from the walnuts so they could finish drying. The skin was tough. You needed a big rock to lay the nuts on and a hammer or another rock to pound the skin loose. The walnut fell out of the skin, revealing still another sharp, ridged shell which also had to be broken before the tasty meat appeared. It was a lot of hard work, but we knew how good they would taste in the winter.

Sometime in September, Uncle Aden wrote Pa that he had a good razorback sow for him if he could come and get her before the snow set in and he couldn't cross the mountain. Pa started off to the other side of the Smokies. He knew it would take him a good day to walk to Luftee. Not taking time to visit, Pa left early the next morning to bring the sow back across the mountain. How do you lead a razorback? Pa quickly found out, you don't! She taught him that a hog cannot be led like a cow or horse. She wouldn't let him tie a rope around her neck, and she had her own ideas about the best way to travel.

Horace Kephart, an early explorer of the Smokies, had met the mountain razorbacks and had his troubles with them. He said:

> Besides man, the razorback is the only mammal whose eyes will not shine by reflected light—they are too bold and crafty. The razorback has a mind of his own; not instinct, but mind—whatever psychologists say. He thinks. Anybody can see that when he is not rooting or sleeping he is studying devilment. He shows remarkable understanding of human speech, especially profane speech, and even an uncanny gift of reading men's thoughts, whenever these thoughts are directed against the peace and dignity of pigship. He bears grudges, broods over indignities and plans revenge for tomorrow or the week after. If he cannot get even with you, he will lay wait for your unsuspecting friends.

As long as Pa kept his eyes on her, she'd behave. The minute his thoughts wandered, she'd run for a laurel thicket and hide. Pa'd get a stick to poke and prod her out, only to have her dart ahead of him and up a mountainside. After losing several skirmishes with her, Pa wrestled her to the ground and firmly tied the rope around her hind leg. When she wandered from the path, he'd give a jerk and get her back on the straight and narrow. Pa and the sow were worn out when they finally got home. Pa's hands were blistered and rope-burned. The sow was tired and mean. Friendship never developed between them. In all the years we kept her, she produced many fine litters, but Pa couldn't go past her pen without muttering slanderous things about her. She kept her black eyes on him and grunted in disgust.

Dorie: Woman of the Mountains

In early fall, Pa and Ma took apples and vegetables to the produce market in Knoxville. The trip there and back took three days and two nights. Sacks of red, yellow, and green apples, and baskets of vegetables were loaded on the wagon. Ma took bed cover for camping out and food and utensils for cooking on the way. They'd get to Boyd's Creek, about twenty miles above Knoxville, in time to prepare to camp for the night. Pa removed the wagon seat and some of the baskets to make a place to sleep in the wagon. At sunup Ma cooked breakfast over an open fire and they went on to the market. If everything went well, they'd sell the produce and get back to Boyd's Creek for the night. Ma always brought light bread and bologna sausage home for our treat. It was a delicious change from biscuits and pork. Luther always managed to get the last slice of bread.

Harvesting, preserving, and canning took most of Pa and Ma's time now. All the potatoes, apples, turnips, cabbage, and sweet potatoes had to be put in the root cellar. The root cellar was a hole dug into a hillside, or just a hole in the ground. It had to be in a place where the ground was dry. After the fruit and vegetables had been carefully chosen, they were put in the straw-lined cellar. The top was also covered with straw and boards. The boards were spaced so plenty of air could reach the bottom of the hole. Bruised fruit or vegetables were never put in because as the old saying goes, "One rotten apple can spoil the whole barrel."

Green beans were canned, pickled, or dried. Some people broke their beans, but Ma dried hers whole. After stringing them on thread, she kept them in the sun for several days, until they were brown and shriveled. They were called "leather britches" and hung from the rafters along the wall with the onions. The onions were braided into ropes by using their long green tops. A lot of beans were shelled and dried. Ma made "soup beans" out of them. She cooked them all day with a piece of side meat for flavoring. Canned tomatoes and corn bread were usually served with them.

Pickled Beans

8 Gallon Crock
Bushel of green beans—broken—makes about 2 gallons

Cook green beans until they change color—from green to yellow-brown.

While beans are cooling, shuck 18 ears of corn. Cut corn off the cobs. Chop three firm heads of cabbage until it looks like slaw. Mix corn and cabbage together but do not cook. Add beans when they are cool.

Use one round box of plain salt on bean, cabbage and corn mixture. The taste will be saltier than you would want to eat. Put mixture into crock. Take outer leaves removed earlier from cabbage and spread over the mixture until it is completely covered.

Put a saucer or plate on top of mixture. A clean, heavy rock wrapped in foil should be placed on top of the dish. Tie cloth over top of crock and let set for eight days. After pickling time, boil the mixture, pack in Mason jars and seal.

Remember, no water is added to the crock at any time.

Cabbage was either preserved whole in the cellar or made into sauerkraut. Some cabbage was put into the crock of pickled beans. Whole ears of corn were pickled, too. Tomatoes that were still green at frost time were made into relish or chow-chow.

After the first hard freeze, the time I hated most, Pa slaughtered the pigs. I always got as far away as I could. When the dreaded day arrived, I'd put on my heavy coat and go into the woods so I couldn't hear any of the noise and commotion. Farm children are supposed to accept this fall ritual as life's necessity, but I never could. It was a gory, horrible time that I would do anything to escape. True, I loved tenderloin and ham, but I wished with all my heart that there was some other way to get food. I tried not to make friends with the piglets in the spring because I knew what fall would bring.

When I was sure the worst was over, I'd return home. Pa had dressed the pigs and Ma and Granny Jane had a roaring fire under the big, black wash kettle. The fresh meat was ready for storing away. The hams would be cured with salt. Sausage was ground, made into little balls, cooked, and canned in their own grease. Ma never used sage in her sausage—just salt and pepper. All the fat was being rendered in the wash kettle to make lard for cooking. Lard was stored in buckets and kept in the springhouse to keep it from getting rancid before it could be used. The little pieces of meat left after rendering were called "cracklings" and were put into cornbread. Nothing was so good as fresh "crackling bread." Ma would have fresh backbones, ribs, and crackling bread for supper. Somehow, in my mind, the meat was not connected to the horrible fate the pigs met.

Pa, Grandpa, and Uncle Dave harvested the wheat, corn, and hay. The wheat and corn were taken to Billy Wilson's grist mill to be made into cornmeal and flour. The husks and chaff made bran for the cows. Ma, Aunt Rintha, and Granny Jane made hominy out of the next-best corn. The corn was soaked in lye water until the hard, outer husk burst and came off. The snowy white corn was washed until the water ran clear. Hominy is best cooked in bacon grease with salt and pepper.

Our cows were very important to us. Fresh milk and butter were prized above anything else. It didn't matter what else we had to eat if we could have fresh, cold milk and butter to go with our bread. Cornbread crumbled into a tall glass and filled with milk was better than the best of cereals now. Warm, yellow butter on a hot biscuit tempted everyone. Honey and butter scooped up with a piece of bread was pure delight.

Milk and butter kept well in the springhouse. Most all farms had at least one small, cold spring running out of the hillside. A small log house was built over the spring, with the spring running directly down the middle. The house had to be built well and all the cracks filled so that the cold from the running water stayed inside the building. Steps were built on each side of the spring to hold the buckets of milk and butter. Shelves built along the walls held all the canned goods and the lard. We learned early never to leave the door of the springhouse open. It was too cold to be comfortable in the springhouse, so there was no danger of us playing in there. Cold air rushed out when the door opened. Even in the heat of summer, the floor was so cold it hurt bare feet. The temperature stayed the same—never freezing in the winter.

Jelly and jam had already been made. Gooseberries, huckleberries, and blackberries ripened at different times during the summer. We went up on the hillsides to find huckleberries and gooseberries. Blackberries grew in pasture fields and open lands along the fence rows. Huckleberries and gooseberries were easier to pick. They both grew on low bushes with no prickly vines. The danger from snakes was not so great. Now, the blackberry briar was something different. It was a favorite hiding place for copperheads and rattlesnakes. Several times, Ma had been up on one before she noticed it. Rattlers gave you fair warning before they struck, but the copperheads were silent, mean, and sneaky.

We'd take our buckets into the fields before the sun got so hot. Dew wet our skirts as we reached and stooped to get the biggest berries. By noon, our buckets were full and our hands were covered with scratches and red from berry juice. Ma would have to remove briar points from our hands. Yellowjackets and hornets helped themselves to our berries. Not all the berries were made into jelly. Ma canned a lot without sugar to be made into cobbler pies later in the winter. Gooseberries were tart and sour. Pa used to say Ma should use all the sugar in the house and borrow an extra cup to get the gooseberry pie sweet enough.

Canning in glass jars was something new for Ma. We didn't know there were such things until we came to Oldham's Creek. Our food had always been cured, dried, or stored in earthen crocks. Glass jars made preserving easier and the food prettier.

Pa had to go to the Glades to buy sugar for canning. Sometimes Lola and I would go with him in the wagon. The store kept a little of everything we needed—kerosene, oil, cloth, axes, mattocks, hammer and hoe handles, patent medicine, candy, and a few toys. While Pa took care of the buying, Lola and I looked at everything. Near the front window, two dolls smiled at us. They were beautiful. We'd never had dolls to play with. Indeed, we'd never seen one this close before. Their black hair was painted on their china heads, blue eyes looked steadily at us, and their red bow mouths smiled sweetly. Their long, lacy dresses covered cloth bodies, and tiny, china feet showed at the hem of the skirt.

"Pa look at the doll!"

Pa looked and smiled but didn't say anything. We both knew we couldn't have them; but, oh, how we wanted them! After we started home, Lola and I begged Pa to please get them for us. "Please, Pa, please—just get one of them and we'll share."

"Maybe, sometime," he said.

We knew not to talk to Ma about them. She didn't see any need in buying foolish things for her children. It was enough if we had clothing to wear and plenty to eat. In a way, Ma was right. We were blessed to have the necessary things in life, but Pa knew how much we wanted the dolls and if he could, he'd get them for us.

All our heating and cooking was done with wood. Pa kept the stack up to a certain level outside the cabin door. With cold weather settling in, we were going to need much more wood. He took the horse and sled into the hills to bring back logs to be split and stacked. Sometimes he took his rifle and brought back a squirrel for supper.

The first snow flurries came in November, with heavier snow after Thanksgiving. Ma and Pa never celebrated Thanksgiving. I knew about the Mayflower and Pilgrims from my schoolbooks, but Thanksgiving was just another day to us. One thing impressed me—the Indians brought parched corn for the Pilgrims to eat on the first Thanksgiving. Ma fixed parched corn for us on cold winter days when we couldn't go outside. The Cherokees had taught her how to roast the kernels brown and crisp.

Pa and Ma always tried to keep enough sugar and coffee to last through a long snow storm. The farm produced everything we needed except kerosene for the lamps and sugar and coffee. Pa was going to the Glades to trade. Trading was just what he was doing. He had taken apples and vegetables out of the cellar to trade for the things we needed. He was gone all afternoon. We watched for him to appear on the trail in back of Aunt Rintha's cabin. Hoping for a taste of candy, we were impatient.

Finally, he came, with several bundles stuffed in sacks on each side of the horse saddle. The sugar and coffee were there and candy for Luther, Lola, and me. Another package lay beside his chair. "What's in there, Pa?" I asked."Open it and find out," Pa laughed. Lola untied the string and the brown paper opened just enough to show two blue eyes and a little red mouth. I couldn't believe my eyes. Too surprised to move, I stood and looked while Lola opened the package and grabbed one of the dolls. The other doll was for me. Pa's big hand reached down and placed the doll in my arms. My heart felt big and noisy, and tears filled my eyes. "Thank you, Pa," I said. He patted my head and smiled. There was no need to say anything else.

Snow fell several times after Thanksgiving, but the real winter weather didn't come until after Christmas. Usually, fair weather held long enough for Pa to hunt fresh meat for Christmas dinner—squirrel, quail, or perhaps, a wild turkey.

Christmas in the mountains was bleak and uneventful. Sometimes the day passed without us being aware it was holiday season. We had no Santa Claus or Christmas tree. Since our Christmas in Spartanburg, Ma had let us hang up our stockings. That was as far as she'd let us go with our celebration. When we did hang up our stockings, we'd get an orange and a piece of candy—never anything to play with.

The mountain people still kept the ancient customs of the native lands. Many highlanders disapproved of the "new" Christmas observed on December 25. In Scotland and Ireland, the day of Christmas was January 5—a day of solemn celebration. Early Christmases had become so steeped in pagan rituals that, in 1647, the English Parliament outlawed Christmas decorations and celebrations. No symbols such as holly, mistletoe, trees, or most of the carols were permitted. Religious singing was restricted to the singing of the Psalms. This was the Christmas brought to America by the highlanders. A carol or two were remembered and sung, legends survived in folklore, but a Puritan Christmas was what we observed.

In some families, the Good Book was taken from the shelf or gently removed from the trunk and the story of Christ's birth read aloud. The carols we remembered were the traditional songs of England and Scotland. The "Cherry Tree Carol" is one of the oldest I know.

The Cherry Tree Carol

Then Mary spoke to Joseph so meek and so mild,
  "Joseph, gather me some cherries, for I am great with child."
Then Joseph flew in anger, in anger flew he,
  "Let the Father of the baby gather cherries for thee."

Then Jesus spoke a few words, a few words spoke he,
  "Let my mother have some cherries, bow down low cherry tree."
The cherry tree bowed down low, bowed low down to the ground.
  And Mary gathered cherries while Joseph stood around.

Then Joseph took Mary on his right knee,
  "What have I done? Lord, have mercy on me."
Then Joseph took Mary on his left knee,
   "Oh, tell me little baby, when will thy birthday be?"

"On the fifth of January my birthday will be,
When the stars in the elements shall tremble with glee."

In a strange contradiction, while shunning all symbolic trappings of Christmas Day, they saw nothing wrong with noisemaking. The men and boys provided the noise for the celebration. They'd go into the woods and shoot their guns at nothing at all. All day long shots echoed from one mountain to another. Some of the more exuberant kept their spirits up by drinking homemade "spirits." Pa and Ma criticized such doings and ignored them when they could.

Many legends and superstitions came to the mountains with

our ancestors. One legend says that on Christmas Eve the animals talk. Bees in their hives are said to hum the melody of an ancient carol from dusk to dawn. The old people say they have heard the music of the bees and have seen cows kneel and speak. On this holy night, the plants will bloom as they did when Christ was born. Although covered with snow, underneath, the ground is covered with soft green vegetation.

Old Christmas, or January 5, is surrounded with superstitious beliefs. On this day the dawn comes twice. The first dawn comes about an hour earlier than usual, and the skies brighten until sunlight seems close. The poke weed sends up sprouts big enough for everyone to see if they're lucky enough to be awake. When dark returns, the sprouts die, then the true dawn appears. Also, the week before Christmas, roosters crow in the middle of the night, trying to make the day come sooner.

You can hear an angel sing if you're willing to pay the price. If you sit under a pine tree on Christmas Eve, angel voices will sing all around you. The price you pay for this miracle is death. You won't live to see the sun rise again.

Wear something fresh and new on Christmas, and your luck will be good. Don't wash clothes on the Friday before Christmas if you want to stay out of trouble. Don't let the fire go out on Christmas morning, or spirits will come and take you away. Don't give your friends or neighbors a match, a warm coal, or even a light to be taken out of the house. If you do, you'll be giving away your hope of a good future. If you leave a piece of bread on the table after Christmas supper, you'll have enough to eat until the next Christmas.

New Year's Day had its own superstitions. It is an old Scottish belief that you will have good fortune in the coming year if the first visitor after midnight on December 31 is a dark-haired person. This person acts as "first footer" and brings good luck and blessings. Eat black-eyed peas and hog jowl on New Year's day for good luck all year. If you hang out a washing on New Year's Day, you'll be washing every day for the next year. Don't sweep out the house on New Year's morning, or some of your family will be swept away from you before next January 1. Never carry ashes out of the house on New Year's Day, or you or someone in your family will have bad luck or death. The same is said for pouring out dirty water. Don't cut your hair or trim your nails on New Year's Day, or you cut your good fortune. It's bad luck to see a red-haired person on New Year's Day. If one comes toward you, turn aside and don't look at him. No matter how pretty your new calendar is, never put it up or refer to it before dawn on New Year's Day.

We ate the black-eyed peas and hog jowl and didn't hang up the calendar before dawn, but we gave no thought to the other advice. Our calendars came from the store in the Glades. They were given out by a patent medicine company that claimed to have the perfect cure for all human ailments. I was always happy to see January torn off the calendar. February was the month of promise. Spring was coming soon!

Pa had a rest during the frozen months, when there was no work to be done outside other than woodcutting and hunting for fresh meat. He cleaned his rifle and made bullets. The rifle and bullet mold had belonged to his grandfather. We sat and watched him heat the lead over the open fire and pour it into the mold. He opened the mold and four red hot bullets fell to the hearth. The edges had to be smoothed and trimmed so that they would go straight when he shot them at a squirrel. All the bits of lead were carefully stored to be used the next time. He kept the new bullets in a leather pouch in his coat pocket.

Sometimes Pa would tell us stories about his ancestors—where they came from and how they came to the mountains. Pa had Buchanan blood in him. He had heard stories of ancestors who had traced their origins back to Scotland. The lands of Buchanan lay on the shores of Loch Lomond, opposite the island of Clarich, where the clan had their gathering place in times of war. The island was given to Sir Absalon of Buchanan in 1226 by the Earl of Lennox in return for a pound of wax to be rendered annually at Christmas. The name "Buchanan" is Gaelic for "the house of

Cannon," and they may have been one of the sacred families of the Old Celtic Church. After the sale of the lands of Buchanan in 1682, the clan spread into England, Ireland, and, eventually, America.

Life in the wilderness had been hard on Pa. He lived with superstitions and fears, which were preserved by the tales told by the older people when they gathered around the fire at night. The Woodruffs were believers in witches and the supernatural. Everywhere in the mountains lingering traces of Celtic-Druid pagan beliefs crept in, in spite of fundamental Christian beliefs. Grandpa John Woodruff was convinced that a withered old woman who lived up the mountain from them was a witch.

Every time they went hunting they had to pass her house. If she stayed inside and they didn't see her, hunting would be good that day. If she was out on the porch drying her hands, they'd get nothing. Indeed, it became a practice for them to return home if they saw her. There was no need to waste time or bullets on game they couldn't bag.

They were convinced beyond a doubt that she was a witch when a series of strange happenings occurred. Several barn cats waited patiently for warm milk after each milking. A huge black cat started coming and greedily pushing the others away, drinking most of the milk itself. Determined to get rid of the cat, John hit it with a stick, injuring its left hind leg. They didn't see the cat anymore, but when they went past the old lady's house, she had her left leg wrapped and could hardly move about. They thought she had been turning herself into the black cat just to spy on them. When John became ill and was dying, he talked about a giant white swan that came to him at mealtime and begged for his food. In the end, he would have to go with the swan to reach heaven. His family thought he was bewitched. Pa didn't believe any of the stories, but he loved to tell them to us as we sat wide-eyed and silent at his feet.

Ma didn't get much rest in the winter. She spent long hours at the spinning wheel and loom, making material for our clothing. Sometimes, when she was in a good mood, she'd pick up

her banjo and sing. "Barbara Allen," "Wayfaring Stranger," and
"Go Tell Aunt Rhoda" were her favorites. "Barbara Allen" is a
seventeenth-century Scottish ballad.

Barbara Allen

In Scarlet Town where I was born,
There was a fair maid dwelling,
Made many a youth cry well a—day,
Her name was Barbara Allen.

It was in the merry month of May
When green buds they were swelling;
Sweet William came from the west country
And courted Barbara Allen.

He sent his servant unto her
To the place where she was dwelling;
Said my master's sick, bids me call for you
If your name be Barbara Allen.

Well, slowly, slowly she got up
And slowly went she nigh him;
But all she said as she passed by his bed
Young man I think you're dying.

Then lightly tripped she down the stairs
She heard those church bells tolling;
And each bell seemed to say as it tolled
Hard-hearted Barbara Allen.

O, mother, mother go make my bed
And make it long and narrow
Sweet William died for me today
I'll die for him tomorrow.

They buried Barbara in the old church yard
They buried Sweet William beside her;
Out of his grave grew a red, red rose
And out of hers a briar.

They grew and grew up the old church wall
Till they could grow no higher;
And at the top twined in a lovers' knot
The red rose and the briar.

Dancing was looked upon as a device of the devil by most mountain folk, but not Ma. She loved to dance. She'd lift her long skirt above her ankles and dance a dazzling Carolina clog. Her feet moved so fast it was hard to see them. Grabbing Luther, Lola, or me, she'd dance around the room until we were out of breath. "Do-si-do and here we go," she'd laugh as we whirled. All too soon, our fun was over and it was back to worktime for her. I never saw Ma sit still very long. Her energy kept her from relaxing in the rocking chair beside the fire. If she sat down at all, her hands were busy mending or crocheting.

Pa looked forward to Groundhog Day, not that he had any faith in that furry little creature's ability to predict the weather. It seemed to me that we'd have six more weeks of cold weather whether he saw his shadow or not. Pa said the groundhog looked for the wrong signs of spring, anyway. If he would come out a little further from his bed, he'd find many sights and sounds promising spring.

Soon now, a warm, gentle breeze from the southwest would sweep across our cold, winter-weary earth, and Mother Nature would burst forth in all her glory. The sun would begin to stay a little longer each day. All of nature would respond to the extra minutes of light. Down under the snow and leaves, wildflowers were beginning to awaken. Across the hollow, the first sounds of spring would be heard. The little peeper frogs were sending out their mating calls.

Ma said the pussy willows were ready to burst into fuzzy little kittens when the sun got a little warmer. If we brought some into the house, they'd bloom early and Ma would tell us the legend of the pussy willow. She'd tell us:

> There is a legend that once many little kittens were thrown into a river to drown because nobody wanted them. The mother cat wept and was so distraught that the willows on the banks felt very sad for her and held out their branches to the struggling kittens. The little kittens clung to them and were saved. Ever since that time, each spring the willows wear gray buds that feel as soft and silky as the fur of the little kittens. Since that time, the trees have been called pussy willows so we would never forget the good deed they did.

Easter Lilies (jonquils) sent up brave little shoots to test the weather to see how much longer they, too, must wait for spring. The cows were almost ready to have calves, and the innocent, wobbly lambs were born on the hillside. One by one, the birds returned. Pa said when the whip-poor-will sounded his first sweet, sad songs across the hills it would be time to plant corn.

Pa always planted by the zodiac signs. The Irish potatoes had to be in the ground by March 17, St. Patrick's Day. He cleared new ground on a rolling hillside and made jokes about his "perpendicular" garden. He said he was probably the only man on earth who could fall out of his cornfield and break his neck. Ma suggested that he stand in the door and plant his corn by shooting it into the hillside with his rifle.

Pa said he had planted his potatoes in rows going up and down the mountain instead of around it. When it was time to harvest them, all he'd have to do was open the lower end of the row and they'd all roll out instead of being dug out. Of course, this was not true, but Pa would look at us with laughing eyes when he said it. We all knew we'd have to pick up the potatoes one by one. Ma laughed and said she'd already noticed the cows had legs shorter on one side from walking around the hill grazing.

The best ears of corn and the best potatoes were kept for planting the next season. Tomatoes were new to us. The season was too short for them when we lived in Oconaluftee. We learned the joy of eating a warm red tomato and a cold biscuit left over from breakfast. Ma would reluctantly pull a few tomatoes while they were still green so we could have them sliced, rolled in meal, and fried.

Uncle Dave and Pa prepared the tobacco bed before the end of March. They built a frame, worked fertilizer into the soil, and sowed the tiny seeds. Cloth was stretched over the frame to protect the new plants from the frost and too much sun. Later, the plants would be set in rows down near the creek. Our job would be to pick the horrid green tobacco worms off the tender stalks. The worms were the exact color of the leaves and about as big as your thumb. I hated this job, but it was the only way to save the tobacco.

Luther learned that the old red hens liked the worms, so he'd call them and throw the wiggly, green things into the midst of the greedy bunch. The hen more adept at scratching and grabbing got more than her share and ended up drunk on nicotine, flopping to one side and then the other. Before the tobacco was cut in the fall, most of the chickens were addicted to the nicotine in the worms.

Our dispositions budded and bloomed with the warm weather. After spending boring, tiresome months in the small cabin, we had the whole outdoors to roam free. Shoes were abandoned, and scratchy, woolen clothing was replaced with cool, cotton underwear and dresses. The creek called us to come and get acquainted again. Dock, watercress, and dandelions grew along its banks. The water was still cold from the melting snow higher in the mountains.

Ma filled her apron with tender poke stalks growing everywhere on the farm. Poke gathering was a spring ritual—because it was necessary for our health and just because it tasted so good. Ma washed the poke, cooked it until it was tender, drained the water off, and rinsed the greens. She stirred the poke and three beaten eggs in a skillet with grease until the eggs were done. We feasted on poke, side meat or ham, and cornbread. We also ate dock and watercress. Nature's garden was ready long before our garden produced anything edible. The fresh greens were a delicious, welcome change from our winter fare of dried or canned vegetables.

The orchard was transformed into a wonderland of perfume and flowers. All the trees were covered with snow-white or pink-white blossoms. Gentle breezes caught the fragrance and carried it into every crack in the log cabin. Our front door faced the hollow filled with apple, plum, and Indian peach trees. We stood in the doorway and absorbed the sight and the smell. When the blossoms were old, the wind blew white petals across the whole farm. We had snow in May each year when the trees let go of their blooms. A white blanket of petals under the trees felt good to newly bared feet.

Lambs were being born almost every day now. Pa would go out

each morning to find the new ones. After his search one morning, he came back home with a small baby whose mother had rejected it. Sometimes a mother sheep just didn't want her baby, and no amount of coaxing could get her to feed and love it. Sheep are, without a doubt, the dumbest of the dumb animals. They wander away from their flock and can never find their way back, they reject their young and are helpless to defend themselves. Anyone who has kept sheep can appreciate the Biblical teachings that sheep without a shepherd are hopeless and lost.

Pa said we would have to take care of the baby lamb or it would die of starvation. None of the other ewes would accept another's lamb. Lola and I fed it in a warm corner of the barn. We fed it every three or four hours for a week. Wobbly little legs grew stronger, and the thin, baby voice grew into a deep, resounding "baa." We'd never been so happy. We had our own lamb to take care of and love.

Church began again when the weather was warm. Aunt Rintha, Uncle Dave, and all their children passed by our house and waved. Pa said we'd better hurry or we'd have to walk to church by ourselves. I thought we all looked so nice in our new spring dresses and shoes. Luther and Pa were dressed in new store-bought pants. Ma still made their shirts. She had on a navy blue dress with a high lace collar. She looked beautiful with her hair up and her soft skin pink from excitement. Tiny gold earrings dangled from her pierced ears. When she didn't want to wear her earrings around the house, she stuck tiny broom straws through the holes in her lobes to keep them open.

When we came near the church, all the children were standing together looking at something. Squeals of excitement came from the group. Lola and I ran to see what was so interesting. One of the children had a bucket of colored eggs. Never had I seen anything like them. They were yellow, blue, green, and red. The red egg was the most beautiful thing I ever saw. I wanted to touch it, but I was too shy to ask. Ma looked at the eggs and said, "How beautiful." We asked her how they had colored them and why.

"They colored them just to make them pretty, I guess. The colors are too bright to be natural dye like we use. Probably something brought in from Knoxville," she said. I kept going back to look at the pretty red egg and hoping Ma would let us color some. "They're only for Easter," Aunt Rintha said. "Some of the children here have been coloring them for several years. It's a waste if you ask me."

Was Easter a holiday like Christmas? I wondered. So far as I could remember I had never heard of Easter being observed like that until the Sunday at Oldham's Creek. Pa always did some planting on Good Friday because that was the day Jesus died. Easter Sunday—the day He arose from the dead—was a more somber day. It seemed to me they had their emotions backwards. It should be Sad Friday and Good Easter.

Soon after Easter in 1910, we noticed a strange star in the west at sundown. It was a big, bright star with a long tail trailing far behind, beautiful and frightening at the same time. We watched it for several weeks before we heard what it was. Pa said some men at the store in the Glades called it Halley's Comet. Rumors of all kinds were finding their way into Boogertown. Some said that on a certain day, the tail of the comet would fall off, set the world on fire, and fill the air with poisonous gas, killing everything on earth. We heard that our earth would pass through the tail on May 19. I wasn't ready for the end of the world. Anxiety filled my life until that day had passed and the comet was on its way to some unknown place in space. We all felt relief and gladness that we were still alive and the comet was gone. No longer did we look up in the sky and wonder if death was near.

Ignorance and rumors are a terrible combination. Having almost no contact with the outside world, we had no way of knowing Halley's Comet was a natural phenomenon and was awaited enthusiastically by people all over the world. Somehow, rumor spreads much faster than the truth and is easier to believe.

Ma had heard rumors about people killing themselves in fear when the sun was in total eclipse. During partial eclipses of the sun, she had seen the cows come home and chickens go to roost.

The mountaineer was as afraid of natural phenomena as primitive man had been.

Soon after the comet left and things were back to normal, Pa returned from one of his trading trips to Sevierville with amazing news. There was going to be a circus in town! None of us had ever been to a circus, but Pa said posters all over town were telling of the dangerous and daring things people were going to do and that there would be animals from all over the world. He was as excited as we were. "I think we ought to go," he said and slapped his knee in a finalizing gesture.

John Emmert, who lived down the road toward Middle Creek, told Pa he could borrow his surrey so we could go in style. When the joyous day came, Pa got up at four o'clock in the morning and rode down to Emmert's to bring the surrey back. Ma, Lola, Luther, and I got up, did the chores, dressed in our Sunday best, and packed a lunch for us to eat at the circus. The sun was still behind the hills when we all climbed into the surrey and started to Sevierville. We went straight down Middle Creek Road into the edge of Sevierville. I had never been there before. It wasn't much of a town—a few houses and stores built around the courthouse in the town square. The dome of the courthouse rose up high above the buildings. It was the first thing you saw. In a large field toward Pigeon Forge, a huge circus tent was surrounded by people and buggies and horses. We felt wealthy to arrive in such a beautiful surrey. Pa hitched the horses and helped Ma out of the surrey. She looked like a fine lady, and Pa was her Prince Charming.

We inched our way through the crowd and went toward the tent. I wondered what I would see inside. Stair-step benches were all around the tent, leaving a circle in the middle. Hanging high in the top were swings and ropes of assorted sizes. At each end, tall ladders went up to a platform under the swings. Soon, the benches were full of people—more people than I thought were in the whole world. To me, a crowd was the forty or fifty people who came to Oldham's Creek Church. There must have been hundreds of faces around me now.

Lions, elephants, monkeys, and even bears did tricks, but the most amazing to me were the people on the trapeze. Two men climbed the ladders and took hold of the swings. They swung out over the center toward each other. One let go of the swing and went flying toward the other man. I knew he was going to be killed. Ma laughed at me because I took such a deep breath and covered my mouth with both hands. I was stunned. I thought my breath would never return. As many times as they performed, I reacted the same way each time. Ma told me to stop it because more people were watching me than the circus performers. Such brave, daring feats were spellbinding. Nothing else about the circus made a lasting impression on me. I was around animals all the time so the horses, bears and the big cats weren't that interesting. We were all physically and emotionally tired that evening. We children went to bed early while Pa returned Mr. Emmert's surrey.

The little cabin near the edge of the orchard where we lived was such a good place to be. In spring we enjoyed the beauty of the blooms, in summer the bounty of the fruit, and in winter the joy of having trees to climb. Grandpa John Watson's orchard was one of the best in Sevier County. He had Winter John, June apples, Early Harvest, Summer Rambo, and something we called the "Stinkbug" apple. It was a little, yellow apple with red stripes, and it developed early, before the June apples. I've never seen it anywhere but at Boogertown. He had damson plums and several other varieties I can't name. Black cherries were in abundance. The orchard provided fruit for several families, with some left over to sell.

Granny Jane, Aunt Rintha, and Ma processed and preserved fruit with methods handed down by earlier generations. Cider, vinegar, apple sauce, apple butter, dried apples, bleached apples, and jelly kept us well fed all year. Whole apples were stored in the root cellar with the potatoes and cabbage. Indian peaches were small, orange-yellow fruit with red insides. They were sweet and juicy and made beautiful preserves. Their origin is unknown and I've never seen them any place but on the Watson farm.

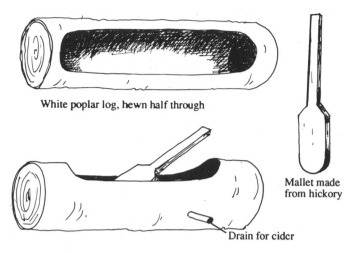

White poplar log, hewn half through

Mallet made from hickory

Drain for cider

Quarter apples and put into log. Then pound to pulp with mallet. Put weight on top to press juice out.

The cider press was carved from a poplar tree, and it lasted only one apple season. Pa always watched the trees so he would know where to find the one for next year.

Cider making was my favorite time. We could have all the sweet cider we could drink. The yellow jackets and bees wanted their share, too. It was a constant battle to keep them away. The men began preparation for cider making several days before. For months, they had been looking for the right size of poplar tree to make the cider press. After they found the tree, they took horses into the woods to haul it home. Limbs, leaves, and bark were stripped from the trunk, which was hollowed out about halfway through, making a trough. Near the bottom of the log, a small hole was bored, with a spout to let the apple juice drip into a bucket. A round mallet made from hickory was used to pound the apples into pulp. When the apples were sort of like course sand, a press or weight was put on them to force all the juice out into the spout. The juice was strained through a cloth to get out the tiny bits of pulp. Fresh cider didn't last long. We had no way to preserve it. It soon fermented and became hard cider and then vinegar. Hard cider can make you as drunk as moonshine.

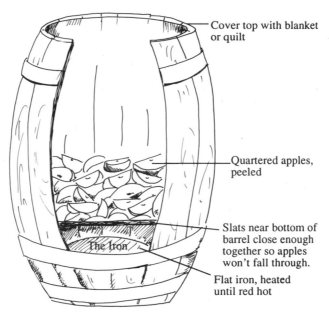

Cover top with blanket or quilt

Quartered apples, peeled

Slats near bottom of barrel close enough together so apples won't fall through.

Flat iron, heated until red hot

The Iron

Put sulphur on hot iron. Vapor from burning sulphur bleached apples snow-white. Store bleached apples in stone jar.

Cutaway View of Bleaching Barrel. Apples from the crockery jar were safe and clean for many months. Mason canning jars became available, but the bleached apples were still kept in crocks. From this basic process the apples could be used for apple sauce or in baked goods such as cookies, bread, and pies. If the children were especially well behaved, they could have slices sprinkled with white sugar and cinnamon or brown sugar; these were toasted in the oven and eaten as candy.

Bleaching apples was another good way to preserve them. A bleaching barrel was a part of the farm equipment, kept only for that purpose. We had to have a new cider press every year but the barrel could be used over and over. While the apples were being peeled and quartered, a flat iron was being heated red hot. It was put into the bottom of the barrel with two or three tablespoons of sulphur on it. The apples were put on a rack just above the sulphur and iron. Vapor from the hot sulphur went up through the slats and bleached the apples very white. The top of the barrel was covered with a quilt to hold in the vapor. After about two days, the apples were removed and stored in a stone jar with a wooden lid.

Dorie: Woman of the Mountains

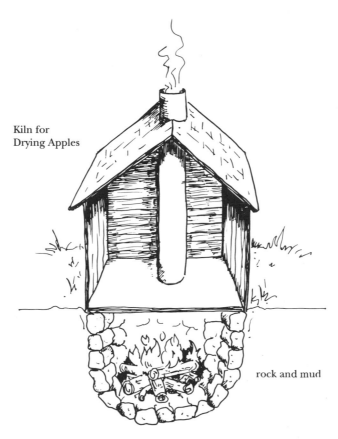

Kiln for
Drying Apples

rock and mud

Kiln for fruit and vegetable drying. Another method of preservation.

Granny Jane had always dried her apples and peaches by putting them in the sun or by the fireplace. Pa's mother, Granny Mills,
was visiting at harvest time. She told Ma there was a better way.
She and Ma built a kiln out of rock, mud, and boards. On the hill
behind our cabin, they smoothed out part of the hillside, dug a
cellarlike hole, and lined it with rock and mud. Over this, a shed
was built, with a chimney through the middle directly over the fire.
Between the fire cellar and the shed was placed a sheet of tin to be
used as the floor of the kiln. The apple slices were placed on it. A
smoldering fire, never blazing, was kept burning until the fruit was
dry. This method saved time and made the apples taste better.

Apples stored in the root cellar stayed plump and juicy until spring. Ma made cobbler pies with them and we ate them fresh and whole. She made stack cake with the bleached or dried apples. Stack cake has always been served in the mountains. The ingredients were easily available to most families—with the flour, lard, molasses, and apples coming from their own farms. It was originally served as a wedding cake. Each guest brought a layer, spread it with apple filling and added it to the stack. The family's popularity was measured by the number of layers on the bride's cake. This was Ma's recipe:

Old Fashioned Stack Cake

1/3 cup shortening
3/4 cup firmly packed brown sugar
1/2 cup molasses
2 eggs
2 2/3 cups all-purpose flour
1 teaspoon baking powder
1 teaspoon salt
1 teaspoon soda
1/2 teaspoon ground cinnamon

Combine shortening, sugar, molasses, and eggs; cream until light and fluffy. Combine dry ingredients; add to creamed mixture, blending well. Cover and chill at least an hour.

Divide the dough into 5 parts and pat into 5 well-greased and floured 9-inch cake pans, or pat each part into a 9-inch circle and place on a greased cookie sheet. Bake at 400 degrees for 8 to 10 minutes. Spread apple filling on layers; stack layers. The cake is delicious if left for a day or two before eating.

Apple Filling

1 quart of dried apples
1 1/2 cups firmly packed brown sugar
3/4 cup white sugar
1 teaspoon cinnamon

Cover apples with water, and cook until tender (about 20 minutes); drain. While apples are hot, add remaining ingredients; stir until sugar dissolves.

The summer of 1911 would be our last one in Boogertown. Dry weather had ruined most of the crops. A few beans and tomatoes in the bottoms near the creek produced enough for us to eat but nothing to preserve for the winter. The corn was about waist-high and brown. There would be no money from the vegetables this year, and the tobacco was stunted. Pa said he'd have to go somewhere else to find work so we could survive the coming winter. He walked to White Oak Flats and found work at Andy Huff's sawmill. Morning and evening he walked the distance between Boogertown and the sawmill. We never saw him except on weekends. Sometimes I'd hear him when he came in and drowsily watched him eat supper in the soft glow of the kerosene lamp on the table. He left home in the morning before daylight and came home after dark. He was so tired that most of the work around the cabin was left for Ma to do. We were seeing hard times now, but we'd never be hungry because both Ma and Pa worked equally hard to keep us going. Pa kept his promise that we'd never eat cornbread for breakfast.

Ma was an excellent manager. She carried a great burden, but she had the talent and energy to overcome almost any obstacle. Pa was easygoing and slow in his movements. He'd sit and puff on his pipe, making smoke rings that drifted up to the ceiling. His patient, deliberate movements sometimes annoyed Ma. She'd complain about him being slow because she was always doing something and always in a hurry. He never seemed to hear her criticism.

When Ma wanted a chicken for Sunday dinner she never asked Pa to kill or dress it. She'd grab it by the neck and give it a fast swing around, breaking its neck. It would be plucked, dressed, and swimming in gravy very quickly. I never killed anything deliberately and couldn't understand how Ma did it. Mountain women had to be strong and not squeamish about anything. I was a complete failure as a mountaineer.

In the spring I had been hoeing in the garden when a baby chick ran under my hoe just as I chopped down. It was dead, and I had killed it. I cried so long and hard that Ma threatened to thrash me if I didn't stop. She scooped it up with my hoe and threw it in the weeds where I wouldn't see it.

In the hot days of August, school started again. This time we didn't have our beloved Horace Williams to teach us. The new teacher was a woman, and a crabby one at that. Almost anybody could teach then if they had a little more knowledge than the students. The teaching position was usually a form of political plum given to some of the more prominent members of the community.

I didn't get to go to school long. One morning I woke with a slight sore throat and a headache. Ma sent me on to school, telling me I would feel better after a while. About midmorning, I felt worse and started vomiting. The teacher told me to go home. I started on the two-mile walk and got as far as Andy Marshall's house. By this time, my fever was raging and I was almost delirious. The Marshall's big dog rushed at me. I stopped still, my feet refusing to move. Cold chills went up my spine. The dog seemed to sway before my eyes. Was he moving or was I? I couldn't tell. His sharp, white teeth gleamed as he drew back his lips and growled a terrible growl in his throat. After a time that seemed forever, I turned and ran back to school with the dog at my heels. I ran through the door and sobbed my story to the teacher. She told me to go to my seat and be still until school was out. My head hurt, and I was hot and cold at the same time. The voices of the children and the teacher rose and blended until they sounded like bees humming.

After school, the road home seemed endless. "One foot before the other, one foot before the other," I kept saying in my head. The dog was nowhere to be seen when we went past Marshall's. Somewhere up ahead was a soft bed and cold spring water waiting just for me. Aunt Rintha's cabin came into view, and I knew rest was just around the bend and up the hollow on the left. Ma put her hand on my forehead and looked at my throat. She said I had a "strawberry tongue" and a rash in my mouth. Ma knew I had scarlet fever. By nightfall my whole body was covered with a rash and I vomited until I felt completely hollow and empty like a shell.

Ma always kept a bottle of carbolic acid tied with a string and hanging from the ceiling. It was kept there to keep us children from touching it. It was very poisonous and corrosive. She put two drops of the acid into water sweetened with sugar. I drank it and lay very still, thinking if the scarlet fever didn't kill me the carbolic acid would. I was so scared of so many things that Ma would get angry and tell me what a silly person I was. Dr. Ben Cogdill came, but there was nothing he could do. "Your Ma's remedy is as good as any," he said.

The vomiting stopped, but my throat was so sore a bread crumb felt like barbed wire when I swallowed. Granny Mills greased my throat with lard and liniment and put a wool cloth over it. The cloth didn't do anything except make me hotter. For five days my fever came and went. My skin was red, wrinkled, and itchy. On the seventh day Ma let me sit up awhile. The skin on my arms and legs started peeling. Soon my whole body peeled—even the palms of my hands and the the soles of my feet. Luther and Cousin Ruth had scarlet fever but not as bad as I.

While I had been sick, all my cousins and Lola had started going to the school in the Glades. We just didn't get along with the teacher at Oldham's Creek. She told one of my cousins to stand away from her when she recited because she had bad breath. Her lack of understanding and her callous talk hurt when we knew we couldn't help ourselves. We had nothing to brush our teeth with except a birch stick chewed to a fine pulp on one end. The pulpy end was dipped into salt or baking soda and used as a toothbrush. Newt Claybough asked Pa to let us come to the Glades, where he and Miles Ownby taught.

Newt Claybough was a member of one of the first families to settle in the Oldham's Creek area. He was a farmer and a school-teacher. He and Pa were friends. One of his relatives, also named Newton Claybough, was a judge in Sevier County before he went west. Miles (pronounced Mi-las) was a member of one of the oldest families in the area, and he too was a farmer and schoolteacher. Both of these men helped shape our lives. A relative of Mr. Ownby's, the Reverend Pinkney Ownby, performed the marriage ceremony for Fred and me later. Mr Claybough was my teacher at the Glades School, and he became Fred's math teacher in Tremont when Fred was taking a course to prepare for work in the newly formed electric companies.

Scarlet fever had left me weak and not feeling well. The Glades school was further away than Oldham's Creek. The walk there and back became harder every day. On Monday morning I couldn't get up. My whole body ached—my stomach worst of all. Dr. Cogdill said I had catarrh of the stomach (gastritis), and I couldn't have anything to eat for a few days. Ma made chicken broth and gave me cold water, but nothing stayed down. Granny Mills and Ma took turns sitting up with me. Ma thought I was going to die. When Pa came home, he took his place beside my bed. Waking from my troubled sleep, I'd call out to him. "I'm right here, Dorie," he'd say, and his big, rough hand would hold mine until I dozed off again. He didn't go back to his job on Monday. In my dreams, I'd go to the edge of a deep, black cavern and then be brought back by his voice and his hand desperately holding mine. It wasn't until many days later, when I started to feel better, that he went back to the sawmill.

When I could get out of bed, Ma took a quilt outside and spread it under an apple tree. Fall had come and changed the hillsides. Sometimes a cool wind danced with the apple leaves and made rippling waves as it moved across the grassy bottoms. Too weak to walk about, I begged Ma to bring my lamb close by so I could play with him. The lamb and my doll kept me busy until Lola and Dicie came home from school to tell me all the news. We did our studying together so I wouldn't be so far behind when I returned to school.

There were only a few weeks of school left when Ma decided I could go back. All the children seemed like strangers to me. I had

Dorie: Woman of the Mountains

known them such a short time before I got sick. Dicie had been a good teacher. I was able to catch up with my classmates quickly.

We realized Pa was wearing himself out with the job in Gatlinburg—or "White Oak Flats," as it was called when Pa worked there. (After a post office was put in the store of Radford Gatlin, a prominent merchant, White Oak Flats became known as "Gatlinburg.") Pa was walking fourteen or more miles on his way to the sawmill and back every day. He got thinner and more tired. Farming was easier than the "hand-to-mouth" kind of existence he had now. It had been a good feeling to grow everything he needed to live on, with enough extra to trade for things like shoes, tools, coffee, sugar, and oil for the lamps, that he couldn't make himself. Hard work was all he'd ever known, but now age and distance were taking their toll on him. Some other job had to be considered. Ma agreed that he should try to find work somewhere else even if it meant moving away from our families.

The Little River Lumber Company was logging in the mountains above Elkmont. The logs had been removed with oxen or horses for years. Colonel W. B. Townsend decided that a railroad could be built into the heart of the mountains if he could find the right men to build the trestles, or railroad bridges. Pa was the man he was looking for. The job would be a gigantic undertaking because the mountains were not the easiest places to build roads, much less railroads, which had to be level and straight. Sometimes the tracks could be laid around the mountainside with ease, but the deep hollows had to be bridged with trestles connecting two mountain peaks.

During the week, Pa stayed at a boardinghouse in Townsend. On Friday he started the long walk back to Boogertown. He didn't get much rest, because there were chores to be done at home before he started back to Townsend on Sunday. We all missed him. We'd watch until his tall, thin body disappeared on the trail.

Pa's dog missed him most of all. Old Shag was a blue and white mongrel Pa had brought home years before. He hunted

Pa, on the far right, begins the foundation of a railroad trestle connecting the two mountains.

with Pa and was always in the fields chasing rabbits or anything that moved. We didn't play with Shag because a man's hunting dog isn't a pet but a necessary part of the animals it takes to run a farm. That dog knew when Pa was coming home. On Friday he'd go miles back on the trail and wait for Pa. If he didn't go, he'd lay with his head on his paws, looking up the trail where he knew Pa would appear.

Just before the school term ended for the winter, I came home and went to the barn to see my lamb. He wasn't anywhere to be seen. He usually stayed close around the barn, because we'd petted and loved him so much he didn't think he was a sheep and didn't associate with the herd. I called and called but no lamb answered. I ran to the house to ask Ma if she'd seen him all day.

"Ma, have you seen my lamb?"

She didn't look at me.

"A man came by this morning and offered a good price for him."

"What are you saying, Ma? You couldn't sell him!"

"We needed the money, Dorie. You know that, and, besides, he was just a farm animal."

I felt sobs building up in my throat. I had to get away from her. The barn was a good place to cry. Nothing heard you except the barn cats and the mice. Cold and darkness were creeping into the loft when Lola came to tell me that Ma said to come home. The lamb was never mentioned again. He was gone forever except for a tiny place I kept in my heart. I felt sad, too, that I'd never given him a proper name.

Oh, I missed Pa! Cold weather was closing in on our hollow, and we had to spend more and more time inside. I hated being inside with no privacy and nothing to do. Sometimes I'd walk around the room and read the advertisements on the newspaper that covered the walls. One advertisement said: "Do you want LUXURIANT WHISKERS OR MUSTACHES?—My ointment will force them to grow heavily in six weeks (on the smoothest face) without stain or injury to the skin. Price $1—sent by mail to any address, on receipt of order."

Another one was: "Dr. Tumblety's Pimple Banisher. Old faces made to look young and beautiful. You may obtain a handsome complexion, exempt from pimples, blotches and etc., by using Dr. Tumblety's Pimple Banisher. Price $1 a bottle. Sent by mail or express to any address."

There were advertisements for miraculous cures for smoking, drinking, sleeplessness, opium and morphia habit, heart cures, catarrh cures, and Dr. Worden's Female Pills for all female diseases. Dr. Worden must have had all the medical wisdom available when

he invented his wonderful pills. It was a cure for all diseases aris-
ing from a poor and wasted condition of the blood, such as pale
and sallow complexion, general weakness of the muscles, loss of
appetite, depression of spirits, loss of ambition, chlorosis or green
sickness, palpitation of the heart, shortness of breath, coldness of
hands and feet, swelling of the feet and limbs, pain in the back,
nervous headache, dizziness, loss of memory, feebleness of will,
ringing in the ears, hysteria, partial paralysis, sciatica, rheumatism,
neuralgia, swollen glands, fever sores, rickets, hip-joint diseases,
hunchback, acquired deformities, decayed bones, consumption of
the bowels and lungs. To be a beautiful picture of health, you only
needed 35 cents for one box of pills or $3.50 for twelve boxes.

What did we need with doctors when the mailman could deliver such wonder drugs? But, of course, we stuck to our tried-
and-true mountain remedies. Ma said there was no need for
fancy pills when the Good Lord provided herbs and onions for
what ailed us. Cabin fever does strange things to a person's
mind. How can I remember all those words?

Always thinking ahead, Ma decided we needed a smokehouse
before the hogs were slaughtered. She thought smoke-cured ham
was better tasting and better for us than salt-cured. Since Pa could
only be home a little while on the weekends, she built it herself.
Luther helped her dig four ditches to form a five-by-five square.
Four smooth logs were laid in the ditches, fitted together at each
corner. Layer after layer of logs were fitted together until they were
about six feet high. With an ax and a wedge, logs were split for
shingles. Pa said it took about five thousand shingles to roof a
good-sized barn, so I guess Ma had to make hundreds for the
smokehouse. She cut and made the door. Inside, the floor was
smooth dirt. A hickory fire would be built in the center, with
smoke rising to the roof where the meat hung. She dug another
root cellar so we could store more of next summer's crop.

When the moon was right—in the dark of the moon—Ma
made lye soap. All year, hickory ashes had been put into the
ash hopper, which was kept in the barn. When water was poured

water

ashes

LYE

Hickory ashes were always saved for making soap in the ash hopper.

into the ashes, it seeped through and was caught in a crock at the bottom of the hopper. The water picked up chemicals as it went through the ashes, making lye (leaching is the proper word for the process). In the big, black wash pot, lard and lye were cooked until the soap was like jelly. It was soft soap, not in bars like today. Everything we had smelled like lye soap. We bathed in it and washed everything with it. The true mark of cleanliness was a slight lye odor that clung to us.

Ma was always busy, but she'd talk to us as she worked. She talked about her and Pa's ancestors and their superstitions. Next to the Hungarian Gypsies, the Scots-Irish believed in signs, spells, and spirits more than any other race of people. Scottish folk were said to have "second sight" and could predict and see the future. Pa had the ability to predict when someone was coming for a visit.

Several times, we had seen him take the team and wagon and go to the train station to pick up relatives from North Carolina who hadn't bothered to let us know they were coming. Pa "had a feeling" when they were coming, and he never missed.

One night, he sat straight up in bed and said, "Owen Maples is in trouble over on the mountain." Pa put on his heavy clothing and went out into the snowy, dark night, relying on a lantern and his "feeling" for direction. He found Mr. Maples hurt and his lantern broken. He would have frozen to death before morning if Pa hadn't found him. We never questioned Pa's ability to "feel" things. He never talked about it himself, he just went on and did what he needed to do.

Ma had her own superstitions. She was upset if a bird got into the house because it meant a member of the family was going to die. Just because it never happened to us didn't lessen her belief. While she laughed at some superstitions, she took others more seriously. If you first see the new moon through clouds, someone in the family will get sick. It is bad luck to burn sassafras or apple tree logs in the fireplace. When you comb your hair, you must not let a bird steal a strand for its nest or you'll have headaches all summer. Always keep a horseshoe over the front door to insure good luck to all who live there.

Ma told scary stories about the White Caps. They were men who rode through the mountains at night, taking out people, beating, and sometimes hanging them. These men wore hoods over their heads so nobody would know who they were. Pa said they would beat or kill "bad women." He didn't like them and said any man who had to cover his face was doing something bad in the first place. Ma guessed that some of those who punished the bad women probably helped to make them bad. I was afraid of the White Caps. I didn't know what one had to do to be a "bad woman," but if we'd had late night visitors knock at the door, I'd have died with fear.

Pa came home every weekend when there was no snow. Christmas was coming, and the snow had fallen every day for a week. We knew Pa wasn't coming home. The trails from Townsend were blocked with snowdrifts. We all felt sad without him.

To help get rid of our sad faces, Ma told us to get ready to go to the store and trade for some candy. Lola and I put on our coats and scarves while Ma filled a bucket with dried peas. We walked in the narrow trail made by horses in the middle of the road. Snow was piled high on each side of the trail. We didn't know how much candy we could get for the peas. It didn't seem like a fair trade—old dried peas for something so delicious and beautiful as candy.

We told the man, "Some of every kind, please." He took a brown paper sack and started filling it with beautiful striped sticks and round peppermints. He didn't wash his hands before he handled our candy. Ma would be angry with me for noticing that. She always told me I was "clean crazy" because I worried about germs so much. She didn't know I never drank water at school because all the children drank from the same dipper and bucket. Ma had no patience with my peculiarity.

Pa came home as soon as the trails were clear. He'd had a good Christmas dinner at the boardinghouse, but he had been lonely for us. So many things were happening on the job, he and Ma talked way into the night. The lumber company was building temporary camps above Elkmont. So many men were coming in to work, and there was no place for them to stay. Colonel Townsend wanted camps full of families, instead of bunkhouses full of rowdy men without family roots like in the Pacific Northwest. He knew families would create better working conditions for the men and eliminate the drunken brawls so common in camps of lone men.

Mountain farmers were already lumbermen of sorts. Their knowledge of the trees, used for their own purposes, made them valuable workers for the company. The remoteness of the timber and lack of transportation had prevented them from becoming commercial lumbermen for themselves. In the 1880s, lumber companies had wiped out the hardwood forests in the Great Lakes region and moved south to the Smoky Mountains.

The sawmill at Townsend was the destination of all trees brought out of the Little River land holdings. From here, the hardwood lumber was shipped all over the country.

By 1890, most of the valuable hardwood was gone from the lower regions of our mountains. Cherry, ash, and walnut were being cut at higher elevations. It was necessary to build the camps and the railroad into the heart of the Smokies. Ironically, most of the walnut wood went to a sewing machine company to build its cabinets. Our timber was being used for a machine we didn't know existed for home use.

Pa and Ma agreed that this was a good chance to make a lot of money. Ma could keep boarders and Pa would have his job on the railroad. I didn't realize that my life was to change so completely and I would have a full-time job helping Ma feed and care for the boarders. Ma said a lot of our cousins were already out on the logging jobs.

Dorie: Woman of the Mountains

III

1912–1917

When I was thirteen, in 1912, we packed our belongings and prepared to move into the high mountains. Uncle Dave and Aunt Rintha were not going now. Uncle Dave said he might join us later. So much of me would be left behind. My childhood was over. Never again would I have the freedom I had enjoyed here in this world of rounded hills and orchards. So much had happened in the last year—my bout with scarlet fever and catarrh of the stomach, changing schools, and Ma selling my baby lamb. Now I was going into the wilderness to face a life without schools or churches, Easter eggs, circuses, or friends. I picked up my doll and started down the road to Aunt Rintha's. Ma said I was too big to play with dolls, and, besides, I wouldn't have time for it with all the chores to be done. I left my one and only doll on the porch of Aunt Rintha's cabin. Some of my cousins would have more time to play than I.

Pa borrowed Uncle Jimmy Maples's open surrey for us to make the trip in more comfort. The surrey was open to the cold blasts of frigid air, but at least we sat comfortably instead of being battered and bruised in a jolt wagon. Every obstacle in the road was magnified many times over when the wagon wheels bounced and slid over them. Men with two such wagons came for our household goods. Other men drove our cattle up through Sugarlands to our new home in the Fish Camp Prong above Elkmont. With the surrey leading the way, we started to the mountains on a cold January morning. We went through the Glades, White Oak Flats, Fighting Creek, and on to Elkmont. Fighting Creek hills were steep. A light covering of snow and ice made the trail dangerous. The horses' feet slipped, and the surrey's wheels went round and round without going anywhere. Pa said we'd have to get out and walk so the horse could pull the surrey over the mountain. So there we were, walking instead of "going in style and comfort," while the horse and the beautiful surrey went in front of us.

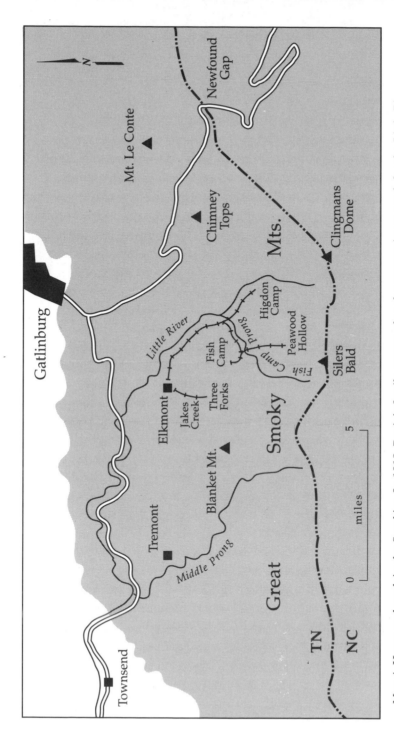

Map 4. Home and work in the Smokies. In 1912, Dorie's family returned to the mountains to work for the Little River Lumber Company.

When Pa called for a rest stop, we were over the steepest part. Looking around, Ma saw an orchard of Winter John apple trees. A few apples hung on the limbs like ornaments on a Christmas tree. Ma pulled one off and tasted it. It was frozen but edible. We took as many as we could reach without having to go through snow-drifts left from the last storm.

The temperature dropped as we went higher into the mountains. Snow was beginning to fall, covering the ground before us and making it hard to stay on the trail. Pa got out and walked beside the horse to keep him from stepping off the hard-packed trail into ditches and holes covered by the snow. Everything looked smooth and perfect ahead of us. Snow had the eerie quality of equalizing the dangerous and the good. Careful, short steps were necessary to keep us from wandering from the trail. Ma had bundled us up in our heaviest woolen coats and scarves. The only part of us visible were eyes looking through the cracks in the scarves wrapped around our faces. Steam whooshed from the horse's nose when he breathed.

Late in the afternoon, I saw Elkmont for the first time. Rough buildings were everywhere. They looked alike to me. Pa found Uncle Harrison Maples's house just before dark. Uncle Harrison was married to Nancy Jane Ogle and had seven children, whom I'd never met. With so many relatives already in the camps, maybe I wouldn't be so lonely after all. After supper there were ten children to bed down, plus four adults. Most of us slept on pallets in front of the fireplace.

Ma shook me awake in the morning darkness. The first train was leaving for Fish Camp soon. Pa had already been out loading our boxes on a flat car. The wagon road stopped here and only the railroad went further into the mountains. It would be our only link with the outside world.

About three feet of new snow had fallen during the night. Pa walked in front of us clearing a path through the drifting whiteness. We climbed into a boxcar and huddled together to keep warm. Heavy, snow-laden clouds dropped down over the mountaintops, shutting out the dawn.

Soon the train stopped in front of a long bunkhouse building. It was high in front with the roof sloping several feet in the back and just a few yards off the railroad tracks. Inside was rough and bare and still smelled like fresh lumber. The cooking area was in the middle of the building. On both ends were rooms with built-in bunks. We would live in one end and the boarders in the other.

Pa set up the stove and made a fire. All the barrels and boxes were stacked inside the door. By nightfall, everything was in place and we were safe and warm in our new home. Ma was baking cornbread and frying salt pork for supper. It would be three days before the boarders came. Lola and I helped get the house ready. We had to have enough quilts, pillows, and soft flannel blankets (these we used for sheets) for eight bunks. The bunks were attached to the wall, one above the other in twos.

Ma's pillows were soft and plump with the down of many ducks and geese. I had seen her take down from them many times. Securing the bird in her lap, she'd hold its legs in one hand and run the other caressingly over the bird's breast. When it least suspected, she would withdraw a handful of down. Feathers from ducks and geese are used in pillows. Chicken feathers have a strong odor that never goes away no matter how long the feathers are aired and dried. Ma kept her feathers in clean ticking until she had enough to make a plump, soft pillow.

Ma made out her food list and stocked the pantry. We hadn't been able to bring much food with us because the crops were so bad. Pa would take the list to the company store about a mile down the railroad. Everything was near the railroad. It was the lifeline connecting one camp to another and to the outside world. At the store, bacon was 10 cents a pound; white flour for biscuits was 50 cents for 50 pounds, and cornmeal was 50 cents a bushel.

On the last weekend in January 1912, our boarders arrived. They were George Rayfield, Harrison Cardwell, Doc Schults, Arthur Whaley, Richard Whaley, Frank Rhinehart, and two Germans from

The Fish Camp store supplied Dorie and her family everything for their boardinghouse that they could not produce themselves.

the Alleghenies. Some of them worked on the railroad with Pa, and some of them were loggers, moving the timber down the mountain to the railroad.

The days were long and tiring. Ma and I got up before the sun to cook breakfast and pack lunches for Pa and the eight men. Pa seldom had to wake them. The smell of Ma's good breakfast got them up. They loved Ma's cooking. She made several pans of "cat head" biscuits, platters of sausage or side meat, eggs, strong coffee, and jelly, honey, or molasses. Ma's biscuits were called "cat heads" because they were big and round like a cat's head. Lunches were cornbread or biscuits, meat, fruit if we had it, and, sometimes, baked sweet potatoes.

I hated having boarders. My days were spent in the house, cleaning or washing dishes. I didn't cook because Ma didn't have the time or the patience to teach me. We washed clothes outside in a big, black kettle. I couldn't go to bed at night until every dish was clean and the table set for tomorrow's breakfast. We didn't get a day off because the men worked seven days a week. They cut and hauled timber six days and cut wood for the skidder on Sunday. There was no church or school for me to go to anyway. Ma's Aunt Rachel Carver's daughter, Martha, lived behind us in a small cabin. They kept one boarder, and Aunt Rachel helped cook at some of the other boardinghouses. Martha soon became a good friend. When we weren't working, we played along the river and took long walks in the woods.

On a crisp, sunny day in March, we were exploring in the woods and came upon the foundation of a log cabin from long ago. Deciding to practice our balancing act, we climbed up on the log frame. Carefully stepping around one of the corners, I lost my balance and fell backwards into the frame. Landing flat on my backside, I lay back on the cold ground and giggled at my predicament. Just as I tried to get up, something furry went over me and into the woods. Looking over my shoulder to see if it had any kin, I saw three tiny kittens huddled together in a sheltered corner.

There had been nothing so beautiful and precious in my life since Pa gave me the lamb. We went over to see if they were wild, but they showed no fear of us. I wanted them all, but the white one with the orange spots was my favorite. Ma would never let me bring them home because they'd be a bother. Martha and I decided we would leave them where they were and take turns feeding them so neither her mother nor mine would be too suspicious of our activities.

"I especially want the tiniest one with the orange spots," I said. "I'm going to name him Muncie." Martha thought it was the strangest name she'd ever heard. Ma had once had a cat named Muncie. She'd never tell me where she'd ever heard of anyone or anything named that. She'd laugh and look mischievous. Now I had a Muncie, too.

Ma loved being near the river. All our water for bathing and washing was carried from there. So many speckled trout clogged the stream that Ma brought up a pan full of small ones every time she filled the dish pan with water. She dipped them out with her hand and put them back in the river. After she put supper on to cook, she'd take her birch pole to the river. She almost always caught enough trout to feed the men for breakfast. Her bait was called "stick bait," a small worm encased in a cocoon found in the water, or red worms. I didn't fish because I couldn't make myself bait my hook, and Ma wouldn't do it for me.

The crystal, cold water took the place of our springhouse on the farm. Pa built a sturdy box, which he lowered into the water. Milk and butter were sealed in buckets and stored in the box. Cold water constantly ran over it, making the milk icy cold. Heavy, green watermelons sank to the bottom of the stream. They stayed there overnight until we feasted on them after the sun started sinking and the boarders felt like having a party. It took three large melons to feed the hungry men. We only needed our "river icebox" in the warm months; nature provided us with an icebox as big as all outdoors from September to the first of May.

Every week new families were coming into Fish Camp. A school was necessary now. Company men were given time off from their logging duties to build a box-like building that would be used as a school and a church. Any denomination could use the building, but the Methodists had one Sunday out of every month set aside for them. The other denominations could use it when there was a free Sunday. Colonel Townsend, president of Little River Lumber Company, was a Methodist, and he did much to promote Methodism in the camp.

Muncie was growing every day and was my constant companion. Ma had allowed me to bring him home if I promised to keep him out of the house and out of her way. She didn't know he waited until the house was dark and came through an open window, finding my bunk and sleeping at my feet at night. He ran like lightning when he heard noise coming from Pa and Ma's direction.

When school started, I left him to fend for himself and stay out of Ma's reach. Again, I was the oldest child in school. Lytha McMahan was near my age, so we became friends. Lytha and her family had moved into the house where Aunt Rachel and Martha lived. They had moved to another logging job to run a boarding-house. Martha took the other two kittens with her. Her ma didn't mind having cats around.

Miss Mattie Bohanan was our teacher. Her family lived at Fighting Creek and owned a store there. She stayed at our house during the week and went home on the weekends. She was young, pretty, and fun to be with. One weekend, she invited Lytha and me to go home with her to Fighting Creek.

We were nervous and excited! I had nothing pretty to wear, and Ma didn't have time to make a dress for me. Lytha said I could borrow her yellow silk dress to wear to church on Sunday. She had two silk dresses because her family had been working with the lumber company longer than Pa, and her Ma, having only one boarder to look after, had time to sew. Friday was the longest day we ever spent. When school was finally over, we all went to Ma's for our things. My clothes were neatly packed in a basket Ma had made of white oak splits. We rode the train to Elkmont where Miss Mattie's brother met us with two white horses to ride down to Fighting Creek. The Bohanans lived in a white, two-story house. It was more beautiful than anything I ever imagined.

All the furniture was bought. The surface was smooth and glossy and felt like glass or china when I touched it. White lace curtains hung at the windows, carpet covered the floors, and flowered wall-paper was in every room. The pictures on the walls had gold frames. I stood speechless and awed by the beauty of it all. The only other piece of bought furniture I could remember seeing was Mrs. Marshall's organ. How could Miss Mattie bear to leave this beautiful house and come to live in our rough, crudely made home?

Her parents were very nice to us. They didn't tease or seem amused by our open-mouthed reaction to such gracious living. Besides the grocery store, they owned a farm and an orchard. They could afford anything they wanted. Miss Mattie didn't need the little money she got for teaching. She seemed to be concerned about the children in our school and wanted to help in any way she could to further our education and improve our self-images.

We went to Gatlinburg, formerly White Oak Flats, on Saturday night. There were a few stores, the Mountain View Hotel at the other end of town, and, of course, a church. Sunday morning I put on Lytha's yellow silk dress, brushed and braided my hair, and we all went to church. The preacher's words drifted over my head and out the open windows. Faces around me were all looking straight ahead to the pulpit. The benches were worn and smooth from long and constant service. How many Sundays and how many people had been here before me? My hands gently touched the soft, silken folds of the yellow dress, which reached my shoetops. Ma had a silk dress for her Sunday best, but I had never needed one before. I was almost a young lady, and I wanted a beautiful, soft dress of my own. Yes, I'd ask Ma for one when I get home, I thought.

Lola and I had a favorite story we loved for Ma to tell. A mountain girl had a handsome beau. Her Pa would let the young man come to see her once a week. The poor girl only had one dress, and she hated for him to always see her in it. She and her Ma decided they'd pretend she had more dresses. Every time the young man came and knocked at the door, the girl would call out to her Ma in a loud voice, "Ma, which dress should I wear, the new one, or the blue one, or the one you made last?" The Ma would answer, "Wear your blue one because it matches your eyes." Of course, the blue dress was the only one she had.

After a big Sunday dinner at the Bohanan's, Miss Mattie's brother brought the horses into the yard and helped us climb into the saddles. He would go back to Elkmont with us and wait until we were on the train going back to Fish Camp. Oh, there was so much to tell Ma and Pa when I got home! Miss Mattie's parents, her home, and her sweetness were lovely memories to be tucked away and treasured. That night in the cool darkness, stroking Muncie's soft fur, I dreamed of silk dresses.

By 1910, before we moved to Fish Camp, the Smokies were covered with logging camps and a network of railroads. There were ten lumber companies from Chilhowee, Tennessee, to Waterville, North Carolina. Little River Lumber Company was the largest company on the Tennessee side of the mountains. Champion Fiber Company was the largest of all the companies, reaching from Waterville on the North Carolina side to the Tennessee foothills near Greenbrier. Besides Champion, there were six smaller companies on the North Carolina side. They were Suncrest, Parsons, Norwood, Ritter, Montvale, and Kitchen. The Chilhowee Extract Company owned several thousand acres above Pittman Center and Cosby. On the other end, near Chilhowee, the Aluminum Company of America owned many acres. They didn't cut the timber but were interested in the water for dams to provide energy for an industrial plant to be built in the future.

People came from all the states to find work here. Lone men came begging for places to stay. Every family who had a spare bed kept boarders. We heard rumors about the strange customs of foreigners in the camps. Ma said Italians, living near Greenbrier, hung their chickens outside to "ripen" a day or two before they ate them. Some of our native habits must have seemed just as strange to Italians.

About this time, the W. T. Cope family of Avery County North Carolina started working for the Suncrest Lumber Company. Mr. Cope was the bookkeeper, and his teenage son worked as a logger. Mr. Cope was well educated according to the standards in western North Carolina at that time. William Theodore was the youngest son of John Alexander Cope and Elizabeth Short. The oldest son was Brady. The story of W. T. and Brady reminds me of the Biblical story of Esau and Jacob. Brady was his father's favorite. They worked in the fields and hunted together. W. T. stayed close to his mother. She decided that he should have an education at any cost. She sold eggs, chickens, goats, and any surplus goods from the farm to get enough money for teachers. So, instead of working in the fields, W. T. stayed inside and studied.

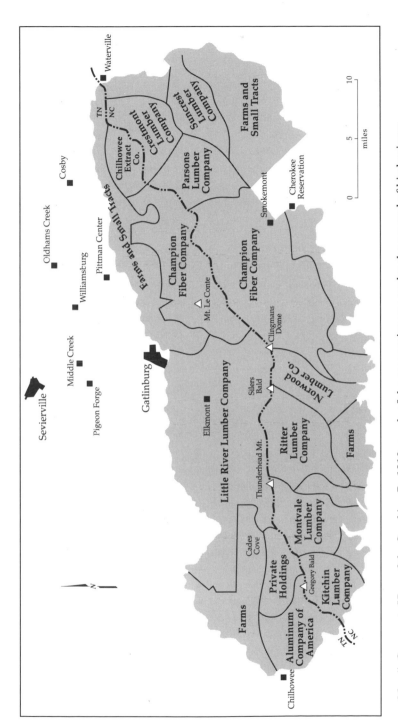

Map 5. Corporate View of the Smokies. By 1910, much of the mountains was under the control of big business.

He became a bookkeeper and a calligrapher. When no book-keeping job was available, he traveled throughout the state teaching penmanship in the beautiful Old English script. He copied official state documents in Old English. These historic documents are probably still in the archives in Raleigh. He married Margaret Alice Key. They were "family tree" conscious. They had traced their ancestors back to seventeenth-century England.

Mr. Cope and his son Fred came to work for the Little River Lumber Company in 1912 and lived near Elkmont. We lived within four miles of each other but didn't meet until several years later. Mr. Cope was the company bookkeeper until he grew tired of the mountains and moved to Knoxville to work for Standard Knitting Mills. They lived on Euclid Avenue in the mill houses.

Fred, their oldest son, had become a mountaineer at heart. He had worked since he was twelve years old. The opportunity his father had for an education was not extended to him. There were ten children in the family and his money was needed to help support them. In a yellowed, old notebook he wrote about his early life. I quote:

> Looking back to the days of childhood I wish to mention some of the things that happened. Some of which I am very sorry for. At the age of five, I caught my first fish which was very exciting at the time. At the age of six, I began selling newspapers. I had to give it up because I climbed upon the yard fence and jumped to the ground striking a large glass jar with my left foot—cutting it half off across the center. I couldn't walk for weeks. At the age of ten, I was cutting stove wood for our cook stove when I stuck the ax through my left hand, losing the use of one finger for the remainder of my life.
>
> At the age of eleven, I did something I have regretted ever since. I owned a mother hen and a bunch of baby chicks. I also owned a little dog. I fed my dog its lunch, and it carried the food toward my neighbor's little store and buried it in the ground. It stayed close by to guard the food. The mother hen and her babies went walking close by. My dog caught the hen and gave her a rough time for a few seconds. The merchant saw what happened, picked up a good size stone, and cast it at my dog. The rock hit her on top of the head and she fell over dead.

My father owned a shotgun, and my mother thought she had it hid from me. I ran into the house, pulled the gun from under the bed mattress, loaded it, and ran back to the yard. Tears blinded me, but I could see the merchant standing in the store door between large glass windows on each side of him. I placed the gun to my shoulder and fired. The force of the blast sent me spinning and finally landing hard on my backside. When I sat up and cleared my head, I could see that both windows were shattered and the merchant was coming toward me like a mad bull. Blood was oozing from two tiny holes on his face. One buckshot had hit him on the cheek and another one on his nose. He grabbed me by the back of my shirt and carried me like a sack of potatoes dangling from one big hand. Ma was already coming to see what the noise was about. The merchant dropped me at her feet and told her if she didn't take care of me, he would. Ma picked up a piece of stove wood and started thrashing me.

At twelve years of age, I got a job as water boy for a railroad construction crew. I began to learn how to use different tools. First was a switch handle hammer drive steel; to drill holes in rock so it could be dynamited; a double bladed ax to chop with; a crosscut saw to cut down trees and cut them into logs; a peavy to roll the logs.

I learned how to drive oxen to pull the logs and crossties. We pulled logs from the woods to the sawmills where they were sawed into lumber. I quit being a water boy and started working with the team when the boss thought I was ready. I was driving a yoke of oxen, hauling lumber to the railroad to be shipped away. We didn't have check lines on our cattle to guide them. When we wanted them to bear to the right we would say "Gee" or to the left "Haw" or to stop we would say "Whoa."

I was standing on a wagon loaded with lumber, moving it a mile down to the railroad. I had to go down a very sloping grade that went into a river. The road had been cleared through the forest and was narrow and rough. I was standing with my feet braced—my chest against the brake. The brake was the body of a small tree cut about six feet long. The lower end fastened into the brake beam. My brake pole broke and I pitched forward, landing with my back against a tree. The wagon wheel rolled against my chest and stomach. There I was, between the wheel and tree, and couldn't get half a breath. No one was near. I thought fast and breathed little. The oxen were very good to mind and do what was said to them. I spoke just as gently as I could, "Back up, boys, back up." They lifted their heads high and braced their front feet, giving a surge backward. The wagon moved enough for me to scramble free. I petted both their broad heads, "Thank you, Lord, and thank you, Buck and Berry." They had saved my life.

Shortly after this, the crew brought in horses to replace the oxen. I helped train a beautiful team for logging. They were almost perfect in a few weeks. The teamsters wouldn't let me work the horses. I was told to build a dam near the logging trail so a flow of water could be turned down it, making the ground slippery and easier to move the logs. When the dam was finished, it was about five feet deep. So, I worked the water flow while my beautiful team of horses pulled logs. One day the teamster came with a "trail" of nine logs, one behind the other. He stopped the team for a rest and talked to me. When he started to go, the team fell into my dam. Their heads and bodies, up to their rumps, were under water. They were hanging there with their log trail still on the path. They couldn't get out of the harness. The teamster started yelling for help and went running back up the mountain.

I jumped into the water, lifted one's nose up with my left hand so it could breath and ran my right hand into my pants pocket. I pulled out my knife and opened it with my right hand and teeth. I cut the ham string and belly band to release the horse from the harness. It leaped up and out of the water. I released the other one the same way. I patched the harness with wire and had it back on them by the time the driver came back. The teamster didn't seem too happy that I'd freed the team. The other loggers teased him about leaving a boy to do a man's job.

There is another place in my memory I would like to mention here. It may sound strange and foolish to everyone else. During the years in the woods when the weather would be too cold or rainy to work, I would spend these days by myself under a large shelving rock projecting out of the mountainside. I would go there alone regardless of how bad the weather was. The rough, rowdy men made my life miserable if I stayed in the bunkhouse. They seemed to outdo each other in telling dirty stories, drinking, and cussing. Out under my rock I could be alone to think my own thoughts and dream my own dreams. I built a big fire and spent days planning for my future.

An education was out of the question. My father came for my paycheck to help support the family. There would never be enough to go to school. So, my desire now was to become a locomotive engineer. I selected my future companion here, too. I knew the color of her hair, her eyes, and her size. She would be sweet and shy. . . .

His years had been spent in the wilderness and a cotton mill didn't figure in his plans. He looked toward the mountains and planned his escape from the domination of his father and the imprisonment of the mills. He secretly packed his clothing in a paper bag, slipped out the back bedroom window, and made his way back to Elkmont. He hitched a few short rides, but mostly he walked. He would let his family know where he was later.

He went to Lytha McMahan's to board. The first time I ever saw him, he was walking up the railroad tracks in front of our house on his way to work as fireman for the railroad. It soon became evident Lytha was smitten with him. She stayed home more, and we took fewer and fewer walks together. He was stealing my best and only friend, and I didn't like it.

One lonely Sunday afternoon, I walked over to her house. They were sitting on the front porch. Lytha was on the top step with him behind her. Her long hair was flowing down her back and he was combing it. We always wore our hair in braids and I'd never seen hers undone. I walked up and stood beside the steps, not saying anything. "Hello," he said, "do you want me to comb your hair, too?" They both laughed. My face felt hot and stinging from embarrassment and rage. "You're a son-of-a-bitch!" I snapped and walked away.

After I got to the railroad, I started running home, my black braids flying behind me. Tears filled my eyes. I'd never said anything like that before. Ma and Pa would use a switch on me if they even suspected I knew such words. I was surprised at myself for the feelings I had. I hoped, desperately, I'd never see him again, but I did. He walked past our house twice a day going to and from work. He was so sure of himself. Even his walk and the lock of black hair falling on his forehead suggested conceit. I thought he was hateful, spiteful, and, worst of all, he knew my guilty secret. Nice girls didn't say things like that, and it haunted me. I had a feeling he was laughing at me.

Dreading to see Lytha again, I worked extra hard for Ma and stayed inside. Lytha liked Fred, and I thought she might marry him. I didn't make friends easily, and I'd lost the best one I ever had. One of Ma's young boarders liked me, but I was too shy to say anything to him. He was nice and handsome, but I spent more time disliking Fred Cope than liking Richard Boles.

My horror knew no bounds when, one Friday afternoon, Pa brought home a new boarder—Fred Cope! He told Pa he wanted to stay with us because Ma was said to be the best cook in camp. Pa had no idea I knew this young man. I felt trapped in a web of my own making. He'd be living in the same house with me, and I'd be serving him meals. He complimented Ma on being known as a good cook. He smiled pleasantly and gave no indication he'd ever seen me before.

Fred wrote his family that he had returned to the mountains and had a good job. Shortly after, they moved to the Greenbrier section to work for Champion Lumber Company.

Mr. Cope started a singing school soon after moving. Money, of course, was part of the reason, but the Copes loved to sing. Along with conventional music, he taught old harp singing. Old harp singing was a mountain tradition. Using books brought from England, Scotland, and Ireland generations ago, they sang the notes of old, familiar hymns. In old harp, each note is represented by a different-shaped note. Instead of singing the words, musical notes are sung. He and his daughters sang in churches or wherever they could.

When Fred went home on the weekends, he sang with them. The fact that he could sing old harp helped his image with Ma somewhat. She loved to sing and went to the old harp gatherings when she could manage. I felt lonely and hated to admit I cared that he was gone. Weeks passed before he said anything to me. Never at a loss for words, he had charmed all the people at our house except Ma. She thought he was a braggart and a little too feisty, even if he could almost best her at singing.

Spring came, bringing warm winds and sunshine. Stubborn patches of snow gave way to a forest floor covered with wildflowers. The trees were covered with tiny, yellow-green leaves. Spring in the mountains is always a time of new beginnings. Almost like resurrection, things that seem dead and useless suddenly burst with life. Nobody stayed inside when the warm sunlight touched them. People idly walked the railroad tracks on Sunday and wandered into the forest to pick wildflowers. Friendly waves and smiles were exchanged. Fred started asking me to take Sunday walks with him.

It wasn't long before people knew we were "talking" to each other. When young folk in the mountains "talked" to each other, it meant they were keeping steady company. There wasn't any entertainment or any place to go. We spent most of our time under the watchful eyes of Ma, Pa, and seven boarders. The men teased us unmercifully and smiled knowing smiles when we walked out the door.

Fred liked to fish. Sometimes we'd sit on the banks of the river while he tried his fishing skills. The water was so clear that every rock in the bottom was visible. The speckled sides of the trout caught the sunlight through the water. They swam close to the bottom and around the smooth rocks. The jewels on their sides sparkled. Speckled and rainbow trout are not easily caught, but Fred usually got his share. It was an embarrassment to him that Ma could catch more fish than he could. He tried to teach me to fish, but I hated it. I couldn't bear to take the hook out of the fish's mouth. It had to be a very painful thing for the poor trout. The only fish I ever caught was a brown trout that was about eight inches long. When it took my line, it startled me. I jerked the pole so hard, the fish went sailing over my head and crashed into the trunk of a big oak tree. The fish was dead by the time I got to it. Fred told me it wouldn't hurt to take the hook out now.

We walked through the woods while he told me about gathering wild herbs to sell. Ginseng and spikenard were sold to collectors who sent them to China. The Chinese thought these herbs were the "elixir of life" and used them for all physical and mental diseases. The demand in China for ginseng was so great that large quantities were sent from our mountains to the Chinese mainland. Galax leaves were sold to florists for use in floral arrangements. The dark green, glossy leaves were beautiful. Neither Ma nor Pa had ever been interested in "herbing," so we never looked for any,

Young people gathered on Sunday afternoons at the all-purpose community center at Fish Camp. Many boys and girls who met here fell in love and married.

other than for our own use. Ma used sassafras tea and asafetida for colds. Asafetida was put into a small bag and hung around the neck to prevent colds. The strong, pungent odor would clear your head in minutes. My cousins smoked "rabbit tobacco," a green-gray plant that grew around the barn. I doubt there is a farm boy who didn't sneak out behind the barn to puff rabbit tobacco a long time before he was old enough to try the real thing. More herbing was done on the North Carolina side than in Tennessee. People in the high mountains wouldn't have had any way of selling herbs because of the isolation.

Peddlers with all kinds of merchandise rode the train into the lumber camps. Red Foot, the jewelry man, came every four months or so to sell trinkets to the boys who had become smitten with the girls in camp. He did a lot of business. For the first time in their lives, people had a little money they could use to buy frills and frivolous things. One Jewish peddler brought beautiful embroidered linens to show the ladies. Ma bought a tablecloth and a dresser scarf.

Fred bought a little gold locket for my sixteenth birthday. I was so happy I shyly kissed him on the cheek. "I have something else for you," he said, "but you'll have to marry me to get it." He handed me a tiny box. Inside was a ruby ring with a small pearl on each side. It was beautiful. "Try it on and see how you like it." I slipped it on my finger and felt like a fairy princess.

My joy was short lived, though. I knew Pa and Ma wouldn't let me marry him. I was too young, and, besides, Ma wasn't happy with the prospect of having him for a son-in-law. I begged, pleaded, and cried until she gave her permission. "Dorie, I was twenty-three when I got married, seven years older than you are now, and I had a hard time taking on all the responsibilities. You'll be sorry," she said, "you'll be sorry."

Fred hadn't told his family about me. I'm sure they wouldn't have let him marry me if they'd known. He knew it, too, and that's why he didn't say a word. Mr. Cope thought they were better than the mountaineers. It was all right to work among them, but marry them—never! They were ancestor-conscious, and we had no records to prove our lineage. It wasn't easy to keep in touch with your family and maintain close ties over the years when it was so hard to get from one hollow to the next. Mostly, our lineage came down to us by word of mouth, not written records. Besides, Ma always said it's who you are now that counts, not who your great-grandfather was. So, facing disapproval from my family and possibly rage from his, we made plans to be married the end of May.

Ma made me a new navy dress for the wedding. The soft, sheer linen was called "lawn." Ma said she'd always heard lawn was named for the city in France where it was first made. All our nice summer dresses were made from it. We picked out a dress in the

Montgomery Ward catalog and copied it. No more little-girl dresses with a high, collarless neckline for me! This dress would have long, puffy sleeves, a "V" neck with lace collars, and buttons to the waist. Six tucks at the waist drew the dress close to my body, showing off a small waistline, which had been hidden under the straight, little-girl dresses.

Fred got the license and said the sooner the better for him. There were no ministers nearer than Gatlinburg. We would have to go there for the ceremony. Pa and Ma couldn't come with us because of the boarders. They wouldn't have transportation after they got off the train in Elkmont, anyway. Ma, less than enthusiastic about the whole thing, left it to us to find a way. We finally decided that I would go to Boogertown on Friday and wait for Fred to come Sunday. We could find a minister at one of the churches in Oldham's Creek, Glades, or Gatlinburg.

So it was decided—I would go home with Uncle Dave Watson to Oldham's Creek. Uncle Dave worked for the Little River Lumber Company, staying on the job during the week but going home on weekends. We hadn't told him I was going to be married. He thought I wanted to visit his family. Uncle Dave was always sweet and kind. I liked him very much and felt somewhat guilty for using him this way.

On Friday, Ma packed my clothes in a basket (the same one I had taken to Miss Mattie's house). My wedding dress and the new cream-colored straw hat Ma had bought at the company store were put in last so they wouldn't get wrinkled and mashed. Uncle Dave came by for me after work. I wanted to stay home until Fred got there, but Uncle Dave was anxious to get started. We rode the train to Elkmont and walked the rest of the way home. I walked along beside him, swinging my basket, with my long braids bouncing on my back. We went through Fighting Creek, Gatlinburg, Dudley, the Glades, and, finally, Oldham's Creek came into view. I wasn't tired. My feet seemed to have wings that carried me along the familiar trails.

Aunt Rintha and Dicie were happy to see me. Everything looked the same as it did the first time I came into this place of rounded hills. The orchard had already bloomed. A few late blossoms nodded to me as I walked through the trees, remembering summers past. Twice, now, Uncle Dave had brought me into this hollow. The first time we were poverty-stricken and weary, coming from the cotton mills in South Carolina. This time, the world was mine. Ma and Pa were making good money with the boarders and Pa's railroad work, and I was ready to start a home of my own. Time, indeed, changes all things.

My cousin and I sat for hours talking about things that had happened to us since our last meeting. She had a beau whom she was thinking of marrying. I told her Fred was very special to me, but I didn't tell her I was going to marry him on Sunday. Somehow, I couldn't tell her my secret. There was no reason not to tell her. Maybe I thought they'd try to talk me out of marrying so young.

Early Sunday morning Fred stood at the front door. He had bought a new suit and hat for our wedding. The suit had narrow lapels and the pant legs were tight around his ankles—pegged, I think they were called. The hat sat firmly in the middle of his forehead, halfway between his eyes and hairline. He looked so serious and maybe a little bit scared. Aunt Rintha thought Ma had sent him to bring me home. He waited outside while I dressed and put my hair up in a bun on the back of my head. It wouldn't look right to be married in school-girl braids. My hat was held on with two of Ma's hat pins. I picked up my basket of clothes and told everyone goodbye. They'd be surprised when they heard about my wedding.

Fred had borrowed a buggy and two beautiful, black horses. To this day, I don't know to whom they belonged. It never occurred to me to ask. I had other things to think about. We were going to Gatlinburg to find a preacher. The day was beautiful. The horses kept a steady pace. A warm breeze tugged at my dress, which reached to my ankles, just above the tops of my new patent leather slippers. I'd never been happier or felt more grown up and pretty.

On the river road in the middle of Gatlinburg, we met Reverend Pinkney Ownby coming toward us on a horse. He was on his way to preach in the Oldham's Creek Church. Fred stopped him and told him we wanted to get married. Rev. Ownby wanted to marry us right on the spot. Fred and I looked at each other. This wasn't exactly what we'd planned. We had hoped to be married in a church or the preacher's home.

"Why not?" Fred said with a smile.

Rev. Ownby sat tall and dignified in the saddle. He reached into his saddlebag, took out his bible and began. We sat where we were and joined hands. A cathedral couldn't have been more beautiful than the setting for our marriage. We sat in a shiny, black buggy pulled by two sleek, black horses. The clear blue of the sky, the soft green and purple hues of the mountains, and the profusion of wildflowers made a perfect picture. Birds sang in the trees, and the crystal stream made a soft, rushing noise. The strong, fast beat of my heart crowded into my ears, blocking out the words that would change my life.

"Do you, Dorie, take this man. . . til death us do part. . . I pronounce you man and wife. . . Amen" I never heard the rest of the ceremony. The timidly spoken "I do's" were carried away in the breeze and the rushing river. Reverennd Ownby must have heard them because he said, "That will be a dollar, please." Fred paid him and shook his hand. He turned on his horse and galloped away toward Oldham's Creek, already late for his service.

We started back to camp. There was no place else for us to stay. Only rich people from Knoxville stayed at the Mountain View Hotel in Gatlinburg. It was almost the middle of the day, and neither of us had thought about what we would eat for lunch. Bohanan's store was closed, it being Sunday. We'd have to get back to Fish Camp before we could eat.

Everything was quiet at the boardinghouse. The men didn't say much to us. I had expected a lot of teasing from everyone, but supper was eaten in unusual silence. After eating, they disappeared one by one. I helped Ma with the dishes and then sat outside with Fred until bedtime. The boarders were still gone, but nobody seemed to notice except me.

As soon as we went to bed, the house was surrounded with men and women. The door flew open, and the room was filled with people. Faces filled the space above our bed—some familiar and some strangers. They lifted Fred as easily as a child and carried him outside, nightshirt and all. Four men had a rail on their shoulders. Fred was put astride of the rail and carried around the camp with much hooting and laughing echoing from the hilltops. After Fred was gone, the women tried to get me up, but I wrapped myself completely in the bedcovers and pleaded to be left alone. They must have felt sorry for me because their attention was soon diverted to helping Ma with the refreshments. Stack cake, pies, and coffee were ready when they brought Fred back about thirty minutes later.

Ma had helped plan the shivaree. It seemed hours before the last person left and Ma's boarders finally went to bed. I felt strange being in the adult world of weddings and shivarees. Earlier in the day, I had been a sixteen-year-old, pigtailed child without a care in the world. When I awoke the next morning, the years stretching ahead of me would be years of homemaking, childbearing, and growing up myself.

Fred wrote his family that we were married. They answered that they were coming to Ma's the next weekend to meet me and my family. Fred and I had the feeling things were going to be somewhat strained. On Sunday afternoon the whole family of in-laws came. Fred's father had a deep, resounding voice that sounded like thunder in the mountains. Ma was already on edge because she sensed their apprehension. I felt small and shy. My tongue seemed to stick to the roof of my mouth and I couldn't say anything.

Our two families had nothing in common. The only thing they found right with my family was our politics. Republicanism was the only thread that connected us. They were Methodist. We were Baptist. Mr. Cope was educated. My father could barely write his name. After what seemed forever, they left. Ma and Mr. Cope were equal in their feelings for each other. One was the match for the other

Fred and Dorie pose for the photographer the day after their wedding. The sober, unsmiling expressions were traditional in wedding pictures.

Dorie: Woman of the Mountains

in verbal combat. When they were out of sight, Ma, with her blue eyes blazing and her face flushed rosy red, said, "I got the feeling they didn't think our little heifer was good enough for their little bull." Ma never cursed, but she had a definite way with words.

We stayed with Pa and Ma two weeks and then moved into the cabin where my friends, Martha and Lytha, had lived. Fred and Muncie were good friends, and, at last, Muncie could come in the house and not have to watch for the broom to come down across his back from nowhere. He slept on the foot of our bed.

Ma gave me enough quilts and bed linens to start housekeeping. We bought a set of plain, white dishes at the company store. A black, cast-iron skillet and a Dutch oven were the only good cooking utensils I had. The battered coffeepot and the forks, knives, and spoons had been "borrowed" from the boardinghouse. I didn't know how to cook, anyway. Ma never had the time or the patience to teach me. It was easier for her to do it herself, and she didn't want me poking about in her kitchen. After my miserable failures, Fred brought home a cookbook. It was called *The White House Cookbook*. All of the First Ladies' pictures were in it, and their favorite recipes for serving foreign dignitaries when they came to Washington. Most of the recipes needed things I'd never heard of and couldn't possibly find in the company store.

Fred thought we were losing a good chance to make some money because we had an extra bunk in the other end of the cabin, which could have been used by a boarder. He brought a Parton man from Gatlinburg home to stay with us. It had been bad enough trying to cook for Fred, now I had a stranger in the house. He stayed a few weeks until my patience ran out.

People were begging for places to stay, but I didn't want anybody in my house for any amount of money. Most people who grew up in the mountains never thought they had a right to privacy. It was a rare cabin that had two rooms. Everybody lived together in one room, sharing all activities and illnesses.

I couldn't do all that was expected of me as a married woman. Maybe Ma had been right about me marrying so young. I was still sixteen, and a part of me wanted to play and be free. More than anything, I wanted to be alone to make mistakes cooking, to read a book in silence, and to show affection for my husband without being seen. There would always be more men than lodging places anyway. Our one bunk could stay empty while I learned to make the change from child to woman.

Fred kept in touch with his parents. They were planning to move back to North Carolina to work in the cotton mills in Gaston County. Before they moved, they wanted to stay a few days with us and try to get us to move with them. Panic swept over me. I hadn't seen them since their Sunday visit to Ma's soon after we were married. I wanted to make a good impression on them. For days I searched through my cookbook to find just the right things to cook. Chicken, ham, vegetables, and cornbread would do fine. For my most spectacular achievement, I was going to bake a cake with chocolate icing!

Fred took me to the store to get all the cake ingredients. Ma gave us chicken and ham. Fred killed the chicken, but I plucked it. Ma laughed at me because I still couldn't wring the poor chicken's neck or chop off its head. "She'll never learn," Ma said. She was right. I'd never learn because I didn't want to learn.

My mother-in-law was surprised and pleased with my efforts as a cook. She had never seen a cake with chocolate icing before. Most people didn't put icing on their cakes. The cakes were usually stack cakes or layer cakes sprinkled with spices and sugar. There wasn't a crumb of my cake left. Fred was proud of me. He smiled and bragged to his family about the good little cook he had. We resisted all their pleas to go with them to North Carolina. The weekend was pleasant, and I felt maybe things would be fine between us since Ma and Mr. Cope would have miles and mountains keeping them apart.

Our boarder, Mr. Parton, was gone. The Cope family had moved to North Carolina, and I had nobody to look after except Fred, Muncie, and myself. After he went to work and I had cleaned the cabin, I had nothing to do except indulge myself. I read everything

I could get my hands on. The lazy, summer days were blissful. Sometimes I'd go visit with Ma, but she never had much time for chatter. I was a true lady of leisure for the first time. Fred was getting good wages on his job, and we didn't have a place for a garden. All this meant I could be as lazy as I wanted to be without feeling guilty. Things had changed for the mountain women. The lumber companies had brought the outside world to us. The men made the money, and the company brought in goods to spend the money on. I would never have to work like Ma did when she was young.

In August we found we were going to have a baby. I loved children, and nothing could have made me happier. The Sears Roebuck and Montgomery Ward catalogues had pages of beautiful baby clothes. I spent hours looking at them and planning the things we would buy. Our baby was going to have fine, store-bought clothes—not flannel clothing like Ma had for us. Fred said I could order a complete layette—dresses, gowns, diapers, everything.

As I grew larger in the middle, my dresses grew tighter. Ma helped me make bigger dresses and large, bibbed aprons to wear over them. Pregnant women were taught not to flaunt their condition. In fact, people seemed embarrassed and uncomfortable in the presence of a bulgy lady. The apron hid my "condition" nicely.

Summer was pushed aside by the cool, foggy fall weather. Some mornings, the mist would be so heavy I couldn't see Ma and Pa's house in front of us. The days grew shorter, and Fred's work hours were finished in the dark. Usually, I could watch him coming up the railroad with his short legs stepping over two crossties at a time, but now he brought the dark, night air in with him. He'd always been teased about his walk. I thought it was a jaunty, conceited stride, but the boarders teased him. "Fred, you walk like a duck in a hurry," they'd say. I didn't like it, but he laughed with them.

One night after the table was cleared, we filled out the order blanks for the baby clothes. Some things came from Sears and some from Montgomery Wards. Everything had to be perfect, so we took the best from both. Fred mailed the letter in Elkmont.

The mail was terribly slow, and our orders had to go all the way to Chicago. We waited and waited for our packages. I was sure the baby would arrive before its clothing came.

Ma had never told me what to expect when the baby came. When the labor pains started, I didn't know what was wrong with me. As the pains grew in their intensity, I walked and walked around the room. Fred knew no more about birth than I. He went to get Ma to come and see what was wrong with me. She said the baby was coming. Just to be sure she was right, she gave me a cup of beadwood tea to drink. It was a painkiller of sorts. If my pains continued, I was in labor. They continued.

The company doctor, Bruce Montgomery, had an office in Elkmont. There was no way to fetch him without going to his office. Fred took the hand-pump car that belonged to the railroad and usually sat off the track near Pa's. The pump car would coast down the tracks to Elkmont, but Fred and the doctor would have to walk back up to our house. The tracks were too steep for them to bring the car back. By the time the doctor arrived, Ma and Linda Gray had everything ready. It was a new experience for Ma and Mrs. Gray to have a doctor delivering a baby. That was something one woman did for another in the mountains.

Tuesday, April 27, Wilma Katherine Cope was born. Ma wasn't impressed with Dr. Montgomery. He didn't do anything she couldn't have done. There were no pain-killing drugs. He just waited for nature to do its work. Ma took care of us while I was in bed. Women who had given birth were not allowed to stand on their feet for nine days. Wilma was a beautiful and healthy baby. I had my own live doll to play with and love. In two weeks I would be seventeen years old.

Soon after, Pa and Ma moved to Three Forks and lived in the bookkeeper's house. It was much better housing, and the company did all the work involved in moving. They'd only been gone a week or two when Fred said we were going to Three Forks, too.

The company rewarded their better workers with better living

Portable company houses dotted the mountainside. They were always within feet of the railroad track.

quarters. Fred was a good, dependable worker, and as his reward, we moved into a movable railroad car furnished like a house inside. It had a coal-burning heater, with the company furnishing all the coal. There were four windows with pretty curtains already hung. The curtains had horses stenciled on them. I thought they were beautiful and useful. Most mountain homes never had curtains because windows were small and set high in the wall.

There were three types of company portable housing. They varied in size and in the number of windows and doors in each unit. Since all portable units had to be moved on railroad flat-cars, the structure couldn't be longer than twelve to fourteen feet and wider than eight feet. Each had a hole in the top and bottom, covered with tin that could be removed—leaving a place for a heavy chain and hook to be dropped through the middle of the unit and lifted aboard the railroad car.

All of the units were built at the company sawmill in Townsend and brought to the various camps up the side of the mountains. They were known as boxcars, cracker boxes, and "shotgun" houses. The "shotgun" houses were scattered like buckshot from a gun blast, dotting the side of the mountain.

Both the inside and outside of the units were made from rough lumber. Tar paper was used as an insulation between the walls. Linoleum covered the splintery floors inside. Most of the units were painted barn red—an almost blood-colored, chalky paint that chipped off easily.

The slightly slanted, tar paper roof didn't fit tightly to the walls, leaving a small crack where snow sifted through in the wintery wind blasts constantly hitting the mountains. When we got up in the morning, the floor and beds would be covered with silky snow. The dust from the 1935 Kansas dust storm blew through and left part of the Kansas wheatfields in our food, hair, and clothes. During the dust storms, the sun over the Smoky Mountains was seen as a red ball, slowly moving between the lofty peaks.

When the house had to be moved, the stove and other household furniture were packed and taken out. After everything was ready, the tin covers were removed, and the heavy chain and hook were dropped down from the ceiling through the floor to steel crossbars that made an "X" just under the hole in the floor. The hook was fastened to the bars, and a crane lifted the unit and put it on a flatcar. The household goods were placed back into the house after it was loaded on the flatcar. The walls usually had a lot of shelves for storage because there was no room for chests or dressers.

The place where the house sat was called a "house seat." It was a pallet-like structure made from poles, which was dismantled and moved to the next site to be used again. House seats were not always used. Sometimes the flatcars would be pulled out on a short span of railroad and left with the housing units still on board.

When this happened, we could be sure the job in that area wouldn't last long.

If the logging operation was to be long-term, two or three units were placed together to accommodate large families or boarders. Doors were cut in the ends so there would be one continuous living space.

Fred was engineer on a skidder, working "daylight to dark" six and, sometimes, seven days a week. There was no church to go to anyway. I played with Wilma and visited Ma in my spare time.

On one of Fred's rare days off, we stayed in bed as long as Wilma let us. I got up before Fred and started breakfast. Salt pork was soaking in a pan of boiling water to remove some of the salt before frying it. After putting the pork in a skillet, I poured the hot water out the open window. Avery Cogdill's bear dog was asleep under the window. When the water hit him, he howled so loudly Mr. Cogdill came running to see what was wrong with his dog. The dog was going around in circles, yelping in pain. I felt terrible about the poor thing, but I wasn't going outside to see how badly he was hurt. Mr. Cogdill was roaring mad. He threatened to come in and thrash me. I was scared because he was said to be a fighting man, and, next to his wife, he loved that bear dog more than anything. Hearing all the commotion, Fred got up and went outside. After a shouting match, they both decided to forget the whole thing. The dog's wounds healed, but Mr. Cogdill never felt kindly toward me.

More luxuries were finding their way into the mountains. Ma bought a sewing machine. We copied dresses from the Sears and Ward catalogues. Our cloth came from the company store or by mail order. Ma no longer spent days spinning and weaving. The store had shelves of calico, gingham, lawn, and flannel on big bolts. Silk was kept inside a glass case for protection. There were chests full of spools filled with colorful thread, buttons by the pound, and pins and needles. Life had never been so easy for Ma, if one can say keeping house for several boarders is an easy life. At least some of her chores were lighter.

Fred and I were at Three Forks for three months before we were told to move to Eldorado. The skidder he worked on was being sent to a new job between Cades Cove and Townsend. The Eldorado acreage was one of the larger holdings of the Little River Lumber Company, out of the mountains we normally worked. It was so far removed that Eldorado is not part of the national park now.

We were not happy there. The people seemed different. There were fewer than five women on the job, and the men were rougher in language and living. I was a nervous wreck from keeping a constant watch on Wilma, who was beginning to crawl and be into everything. My every move seemed to be watched by the timber-cutting crews working close to the cabin.

Fred's hunting dog, Jake, wasn't happy either. There was no time for hunting, and somebody was always telling him to get out of the way. The final straw was when Fred scolded him for eating food a neighbor had put out for his pigs. Old Jake couldn't take it anymore. He left and went back home to Three Forks. He showed up at Ma and Pa's, lean and hungry. Ma wrote that he had come home.

I was homesick, too, I knew exactly how Jake must have felt. Fred agreed that Wilma and I would be happier back with the family. He spent the last three months in Eldorado by himself.

Eldorado was named by a mountain man who had journeyed to the far West in search of gold. After not finding any there, he became convinced there was gold in the Smokies. He came back and created his own western town—Eldorado. It had a different feeling than the other places we lived. Maybe he did bring part of the Old West with him.

The kind of gold he was looking for couldn't be found in our mountains. Most of life's true gold is missed by people who look down for shiny, yellow pieces of metal instead of up at the golden beauty of a mountain sunset, the golden wildflowers, and the simple gold that forms on the churn dasher as cream turns into golden mounds of butter.

Our job in Eldorado was over in six months and there wouldn't be another one until early spring. Ma and Pa asked us to live with them until Fred could work again. The bookkeeper's house was big and warm. Ma still kept boarders, so we could earn our keep by helping her with the work. Ma had kept Muncie for me. He was thin and sad when I saw him again.

Before going to Three Forks for the winter, we decided to go to Cramerton, North Carolina, to see Fred's family. Wilma was less than a year old when she crossed the mountains for the first time. The train had a dining car but no sleepers. We would have to sit up all night in the passenger car. The conductor came down the aisle saying supper was being served in the dining car.

The tables had red checked cloths, snow-white dishes, and silverware. Beside each plate was a small crystal bowl filled with water. I didn't know what they were for, and Fred didn't either. While we waited for our food, Fred became thirsty. "I guess we're suppose to drink this," he said. He did. Later we noticed other people dipping their fingers into the bowls and drying them on their napkins. Fred looked embarrassed. "They're finger bowls," he whispered. "I hope nobody saw me drink mine." The waiter noticed the empty bowl and gave Fred a sad, sorrowing look. We laughed about it when we were safely out of the dining car. "Live and learn," he laughed.

We had a good time with the Copes. They spoiled Wilma dreadfully. Several members of the family were working in the mills and money was no problem. In fact, they were doing so well that they begged us to stay and work. One of the great sadnesses of their lives was losing Fred to a Tennessee girl who had no intentions of leaving the mountains. We both wanted to return to the Smokies, so the pleading was in vain. After a week, we boarded the train to take us back to Three Forks.

Three Forks was covered with several feet of snow when we got back. The lumber business was at a midwinter standstill. Pa and the boarders hunted and fished and exchanged tall tales while they waited for a break in the weather. Pa woke bright and cheerful one Sunday morning and challenged Fred to catch as many fish as he could. They were out all morning. At noon they came home with eighteen fish. Fred had caught fifteen, and Pa had three. Pa couldn't let him win, so he challenged him again. They were out until supper. Again they brought in eighteen fish. Fred had fifteen and Pa had three. Pa said it just hadn't been a good day to fish. There was a time when they caught 128 trout in four hours, enough for a meal for all the neighbors. Ma was surprised that time. She could outfish them both. "The fish must have died from shock," she said.

When all the trains and machinery were quiet, we could hear the sudden rumble of an approaching earthquake. We felt tremors all over the mountains. Just at supper time in 1916, a quake shook the house, jarring dishes off the shelves. The table danced around, bumping into us as we sat around it. As soon as we realized what was happening, we ran outside until the tremor was over. It only lasted a few minutes, but it seemed like hours. We stayed together in one room, expecting another quake to follow. Pa and Fred went to see if any of our neighbors had suffered damage. A man told Pa that Dr. Montgomery's office was in shambles. All the medicine stored on shelves was broken and scattered over the floor. Other than fire on the mountain, earthquakes were the most feared.

Even with quakes and flash floods, we lost relatively few people. Minor train accidents were frequent, but we didn't hear of many deaths or severe injuries. Charles Badgett, superintendent of the Little River Lumber Company, invited his father to spend the day on the job with him. They were riding in the caboose with the train crew, behind a long string of flatcars. The caboose broke loose and started back down the track. Mr. Badgett and his father jumped off the caboose. The elder Mr. Badgett was killed, along with Pleas Myers and Earl Dockery. All the crew had jumped from the runaway car except my Uncle John Hampton. He didn't get a scratch, while the others suffered severe cuts and bruises. The caboose went about a mile down the mountain and jumped the tracks, going into the river. Uncle John walked back up the railroad. He said he knew the caboose would have to stop somewhere,

Train wrecks were frequent and often fatal. Three men died in this wreck. Dorie's uncle, John Hampton, survived the impact.

and he'd just ride it out. Besides, he said he was too scared to move, much less jump.

In April of 1916, the Peawood Hollow job started. We moved back into our movable railroad car and went higher into the mountains. Pa and Ma stayed at Three Forks with the boarding-house. The winter had been a mild one, and spring arrived early. Everything was green and lush in Peawood Hollow. The mountains were straight up and down all around us. Certainly there would be no place for a garden, and the cow would have to be stabled up on the mountain. The only level places were beside the railroad where our house would be sidetracked. Men had labored for months digging a bed for the tracks around the mountain. Our house would only be a few feet from the railroad.

We were stuck on the side of the mountain like bugs on flypaper. Just behind the house, the earth stopped and plunged into a deep hollow. The sides were straight up and down, seem-ingly without a bottom. Men struggled to get the logging equip-ment on the mountain. The train made many groaning, agoniz-ing trips in front of our house. The skidder was pushed and pulled

Fred and Dorie show off their baby, Wilma Katherine, outside their home in Peawood Hollow. Dorie is wearing Fred's white hat.

Dorie: Woman of the Mountains

into place. I could hear the train's wheels spinning on the tracks as it strained to do its work.

One evening, after we'd been there a few weeks, the dark mountain shadows were moving toward the house, and in the failing light, I saw a small animal coming up the railroad. Assuming it was an opossum or raccoon, I thought no more about it until I heard scratching at the door. "What is it?" and "Is it mad with rabies?" were my thoughts. The scratching continued, and then I heard a gentle "meow." Slightly opening the door enough to see what it was, I heard the "meow" again. Now, I knew what it was. There stood Muncie asking politely to come inside.

Only God knew how he had found me. We were sixteen miles away from where I'd left him with Ma. There were a mountain and a river between us. Had he followed a star to find his way as the early sailors had done to find their way across oceans? Thankful for whatever instinct that had urged him on, he was home, and I was overjoyed. To use Fred's words, he was "razor-soup" thin and very tired. His sweet, but somewhat goofy, face gazed up at me and loud, rumbly purrs told us how happy he was to be home again. I'd never leave him with anyone else.

Soon everything was running, and loads of logs rumbled by the house. The weight and movement of the trains jarred the earth. Dishes rattled and sometimes tumbled to the floor. Wilma had to be watched constantly. The trains and the deep hollow made this a dangerous place for a child. She had to stay inside unless I was with her.

We hadn't been there long when a log train, going past with a loader full of logs, fell over directly in front of our house. It barely missed the house and fell over the side of the mountain. The whole thing was over before I realized what had happened. I heard the metallic, squeaky noise of the train, the thunderous boom of the logs hitting the ground, and then silence as they fell into the hollow.

Loaders are equipped with boilers of their own to produce power. Looking out the door, I saw the loader lying on its side with hot, white steam hissing. Thinking it would explode any minute, I grabbed Wilma and ran up the tracks, away from the wreck. The crew met me on their way down. They said there wasn't any danger of explosion and I could stay in the house. Wilma, sensing my terror, was screaming at the top of her voice. Two cranes were brought up from Elkmont to pull the loader back on the tracks. A few more feet and it would have been in the deep hollow with the logs.

Fred still worked the dawn-to-dusk shift while I took care of things at home. We had four boarders, who had to be fed morning and night and have lunches packed for the job. I had to carry water from a spring about a half mile away for all our drinking, cooking, and washing. Once a week, I made out a grocery list and sent it out on the train to the company store.

After all the men were gone, Wilma and I were free to do what we wanted. Morning and evening, we climbed the mountain to milk the cow. She grazed around the house and up the mountain, always returning to her stall for milking time. She waited in the stall until we came to milk. One morning she wasn't anywhere to be seen. Calling and looking, we went around the mountain. Wilma pointed down to the hollow below. The cow never went there, so I kept calling. "Mama," Wilma said, "she's down there." I looked down. The cow was there all right—dead. She had fallen off the mountain and broken her neck.

The death of our cow was a great loss, and I didn't know how we would replace her. I thought of the jokes Pa and Ma used to make about falling out of the cornfield. What would they say about our cow falling out of her pasture?

Just before Easter, I decided I wanted to color eggs for Wilma. The store in Elkmont didn't have any. Fred said he needed to go to the Sugarlands to buy another cow and he'd try to get some there. He bought the cow and twelve dozen eggs. When his check was cashed, he was paid in gold coins. Money is money, after all, and we didn't realize that one day those coins would be very valuable.

Fred Cope, Dave Gray, and Commodore Gilland (*left to right*) operate a skidder, which piled logs awaiting the train and the loader. The machine was steam powered, using coal for energy.

The cow was put in the stall and the eggs were brought into the house. Twelve dozen eggs add up to 144 eggs. Actually, there was a crate full of beige eggs. I asked Fred what I was supposed to do with all of them. "Boil 'em and eat 'em," was his reply. I didn't know whether to laugh or cry. He, at least, had bought the fancy dye, and Wilma would have pretty eggs like the ones I saw at Oldham's Creek Church years before.

I boiled and colored 24 eggs—a dozen for Wilma and some for the boarders on Easter morning. That only left me 120 to use be-

Following the skidder, the loader lifted the logs to a flatbed railroad car to be taken to the sawmill. A loader like this overturned in front of the Cope's house and the logs fell off the mountain.

fore they spoiled. For a week, we had eggs at every meal, and I felt if I never saw another one, it would be too soon. The grocery lists I sent out with Fred were more specific after that.

Fred also bought a high-powered rifle to use for hunting and for protection. Up to this time, we'd never had a gun. Pa still had his shotgun and a rifle. Pa had a liking for squirrel and gravy. He went hunting when he had spare time. When Pa was sick, Ma had one of the boarders or Luther go kill a squirrel so she could make soup or gravy and restore Pa to his original good health. Fred was more of a fisherman than a hunter. His hunting ability wouldn't have kept meat on our table.

In the fourth and final stage of logging, what were once tall trees are on their way to Townsend to be processed into lumber.

Peawood Hollow was beautiful. Wilma and I walked along the railroad and picked wild strawberries and flowers. There were large patches of orange and black tiger lilies, more than I ever saw anywhere. Ramps grew in the loose, fertile soil. Every time we wanted some to go with our cornbread and soup beans, we could reach out the back door and pull them up. I should say the boarders ate the ramps. I never learned to like them.

I wasn't afraid to live in such a remote place. I did miss having other women to talk with. Whenever we could, we went to Three Forks to visit Pa and Ma. Most of our early family pictures were made there. A photographer came regularly to keep our family album up to date. Anyway, I was learning self-reliance while perched on the side of the Smokies in Peawood Hollow. Ma had taught me home remedies for most ailments. Our mountain medicine was as effective as any given by the doctors we'd had contact with so far. If illness came, we handled it with herbs and prayer. We were a sturdy, hearty group of people. Our ancestors had to have exceptional health to survive in the mountains.

Granny Jane Watson was bitten on her right hand by a copperhead one summer, when she was scratching potatoes out of the hard, dry dirt in the garden. The potatoes had grown extra large that year and had pushed the dirt up, leaving cracks in the soil around them. She ran to the house and made an "X" cut on her finger where the bite was, and, with a milking motion, caused it to bleed as much as it would. By the time Ma found her, her hand was bright red and swollen almost twice the size it should be. Granny Jane told her to mix cornmeal and lye soap together and make a poultice for her hand. As the poultice dried, it drew out the poison. Her hand turned blue by morning, but they kept changing poultices as they dried, and in a few days she was in good health.

Fred kept a half gallon jar of "white lightning" or "moonshine" whiskey. We mixed it with honey for sore throats and colds. It was good for cuts and bruises, too. A lot of misunderstanding has arisen over the mountaineer's whiskey still. In Scotland, each family or clan had a still to produce the whiskey used for medicinal purposes and a little extra for holiday "spirits." It was a disgrace for a Highlander to be a drunk. They knew and respected the potency of home brew. Herbs and home brew were all they had to treat sickness.

This tradition was handed down through the years, and mountaineers couldn't understand why it became illegal to own and operate a family still. They didn't believe it was wrong to distill the grain from their fields and the fruit from their orchards. Their ancestors had done it—an honorable and long-standing practice, a custom and skill, as much a domestic right as baking their own bread.

Trouble came after the government levied a tax against the distillers. Having come through a war battling "taxation without representation," the Highlanders were angered over the government interference in family business. Thomas Jefferson, as president, had repealed the tax on alcohol made in the southern mountains, and it stayed tax-free until 1862. The federal tax on a gallon of whiskey was twenty cents. The tax rose steadily until 1864, when it leaped to two dollars a gallon—money that no mountaineer had.

About this time, the term "moonshine" came into being. In order to escape the taxes and the revenue collectors, the mountaineers started brewing their spirits by moonlight. They were constantly moving their distilling equipment, looking for new coves where the telltale wisps of smoke wouldn't betray them. Mind you, the government didn't mind if whiskey was made, so long as they got their share of the money. True mountaineers usually made enough for their own family use and wouldn't sell it. No one in my family made whiskey, but we had friends and neighbors who shared theirs with us when we needed it for medicinal purposes. No money changed hands.

The season passed quickly. The job here was almost done. Fred hadn't been told where we would go next. No place could be more remote and hazardous than Peawood Hollow. Almost any place would be better for raising babies. I was pregnant again, and this time we hoped for a boy. "We'll name him Paul after the Apostle Paul," Fred said. "Maybe he'll be a preacher."

My appetite increased along with my waistline. Out came the bibbed aprons to cover my "condition" and make me presentable. Fred was always looking for small game so I could have fresh meat. The only meat at the company store was bacon, ham, or sidemeat. I got so tired of pork. I craved chicken. We hadn't had much fish since we left Three Forks. The river was at the bottom of my "bottomless" hollow. My taste buds longed for a taste of the jeweled, sleek trout swimming among the rocks, completely out of my reach.

Just at dusk, we were sitting on the front steps watching the last rays of the sun disappear behind the mountain. A pheasant sailed slowly over the house and sat in the top of an oak. Fred got his rifle and shot at the bird. It fell to the ground. Bragging about his expert marksmanship, he picked up the pheasant but couldn't find a bullet hole. There was a tiny, bare spot on the head. Either the bullet had grazed its head, causing a concussion, or the poor thing died of fright. Fred cleaned and dressed it while I got out my biggest kettle. I was going to have dumplings!

The thought of fluffy, white dumplings floating in rich, golden broth, filled my dreams all night. First thing in the morning, I put the bird on the back of the stove to cook all day. At midmorning, I tried to stick a fork into it to test for tenderness, but it was like an old shoe. At noon, it was still the same. I put more wood in the stove and added an onion. That's what Ma did to make a tough, old bird tender. "A watched pot never boils," Ma always said. I decided not to look at the bird again until supper time.

I burned all the wood in the house, keeping the water boiling in the kettle. Just before supper, I prepared flour, lard, and milk to be turned into my dumplings. I slowly opened the lid to peek at the bird. It looked exactly as it did at noon. The fork wouldn't go through the skin. There was no broth, only oniony-smelling water. It never got tender enough to eat. "The poor old thing probably died with a heart attack," Fred said.

The men were working their way back down the mountain. We were moved two miles out of the hollow, near Higdon Camp. We lived there about three months until winter set in. We again moved in with Pa and Ma at Three Forks. Muncie was getting accustomed to riding in a basket.

In January 1917, an earthquake rocked the mountains. The tremor seemed to start in the center of the mountains and gained strength as it reached outward to Wear's Valley. The house swayed and the window panes popped out of their frames, shattering as they hit the floor. We grabbed what we could to wrap up in, against the January weather. We stayed outside until the tremor moved away from us. The aftershocks came in waves, growing weaker with each wave. In the morning, Pa went to the spring for water to prepare breakfast. He came back with an empty bucket. "The spring is running muddy water as thick as syrup," he said. We used river water until the spring ran clear again.

Higdon Camp was on Three Forks just above Elkmont, high in the mountains below Clingman's Dome. It had been named for Lee Higdon who lived in the possession cabin belonging to the Little River Lumber Company.

It was common practice for men to be paid by the company to live in cabins on land the company was claiming through legal occupancy. Most of the lumber companies used this method to secure thousands of acres of land for timber cutting. The Little River Lumber Company had a special representative known as a land agent, surveyor, and title man. He knew where the possession cabins were and how much land was included in the claim. He made regular visits to the cabins and filed reports back to the home office in Townsend.

Mountain people seldom bothered to make legal claims or documentation on their property. If a deed or ownership of land was questionable, the company could build a possession cabin, have somebody live in it several days a month, maintain a small garden or orchard for seven years, and the occupancy was not questioned—the land became theirs.

If no deed or claim existed, it took twenty years of legal occupancy to take the land. Only one incident is known where a company cabin was reclaimed by the former resident. A Mrs. McClanahan found an empty possession cabin on her property in Blount County. She broke open the door and turned the house over to Bell McCampbell. This was in 1915, and Bell McCampbell was still in the house in 1921. She and the company finally came to a verbal agreement, and they let her stay in the house.

Higdon Camp was going to be the center for a logging job that was about three times bigger than their normal range. Men and equipment were brought in for weeks. Pa and Ma were in charge of the boardinghouse. Fred and I gave up the railroad-car house and moved in with them to help work. There would be eight men living in the house besides us. It was up to Ma and me to cook and take care of them. Pa still worked on the railroad and Fred was running a skidder.

About a hundred boxcar houses were scattered on both sides of the river. These houses were almost square in shape, made of tar paper and rough lumber and, of course, owned by the company. Several large families had more than two units to give them much needed space. The units were not very stable. Earthquakes and strong winds would separate them. It was unnerving to have your house come apart.

Fires were always a threat anywhere there were people. The railroad created a severe problem. Flying sparks from trains set many small fires along the tracks. Sparks and cinders belched out of the smokestack, covering the cars behind the engine. Even in the passenger cars, the cinders fell on our heads and clothing. Any wisp of smoke in the woods caused concern.

The fire in 1917 was started somewhere along the cutting line— perhaps from a skidder's tinder box. A small cinder flickered to life, igniting the leaves and debris. Trees lit up like Roman candles. Flames ate through the underbrush and swooshed up the trees, trapping the men higher on the mountain. They ran for any break they could find and out toward the camp. They thought the camp might have already been burning.

Fred was trapped behind a searing wall of fire. He had no place to run. The fire was going up the mountain faster than he could run. Smoke and heat were already affecting his mind. He put his hands over his face and prayed. When he raised his head, a small break opened in the fire wall and he dashed through to safety.

Winds were driving the flames along the treetops, gathering heat and speed as they went. Trees were exploding, sending fiery debris sailing through the air into the virgin timber. Smoke filled the sky with a gray-black ceiling. It rolled into camp in waves. Our lungs and eyes stung from the thick, heavy fumes still hot from the blaze.

All the men made it back to camp and started the evacuation. Fred bolted through the door, out of breath, covered with dirty stains of smoke and soot and wet with sweat from the intense heat and fear. Looking around, he saw we were all safe. He went limp and fell against the door while tears of relief fell down his cheeks. His body shook with great sobs. I had never seen him cry before. His self-assured, jaunty shell had been cracked. At that moment, I knew how much we meant to him, without him saying a word.

After a headcount, to see if everyone was accounted for, anyone who wanted to leave could take the train out of the danger area. It would make several trips before all the people could go. The fire was burning out of control, and the wind was turning it in the direction of the camp. Pa and Ma said they wanted to stay and try to save all their belongings. For the first time, they had things worth saving and couldn't bear to leave them behind. We decided to stay with them. All eight boarders stayed to help save the house.

We all joined the bucket brigade. It would take a lot of water to keep the sparks from igniting the tar paper roof. Wilma was our main concern. The river was very near. We thought we would be safe in the water if the worst happened. Houses on the upper end of the camp were already burning. We got all the buckets, pots, and pans to bring water from the river to pour on our roof. About a half mile above us, Harrison Watson took everything out of his house and put it on the rocks in the middle of the river, thinking it would be safe there.

Smoke covered the sun. The only light was an eerie, orange glow from the flames. The fire was coming closer, we could hear the hissing sound of sap boiling. Pine needles shot like fiery darts when flames engulfed the tree. Above us, the roar of tornado-like winds and exploding trees echoed throughout the mountains. All night, buckets of water were poured over the roof and sides of the house. Wilma slept short, fretful naps. The room was hot and steamy, too uncomfortable for her to sleep. When she woke, she clung to my skirt and sobbed. My clothes were soaked from river water and perspiration. I ached all over, and I couldn't feel the buckets in my hand anymore. Vaguely, I thought about my un-born baby and wondered if this horror could cause it to be born too soon.

Just before dawn, the wind changed again and swept the fire back up the mountain, away from the camp. We were safe now. The air was heavy and hard to breathe, but we were safe. I lay down on the bed but I couldn't feel it under me. My whole body must have been numb. Pa said we'd better rest while we could because fire and wind are unpredictable. We got a little sleep before facing the reality of what morning would bring.

The sunlight looked pale and weak when we got up. Smoke hung over the camp. The air smelled of charred timber. Higdon became a ghost town overnight. Pa and Fred went to see if anyone needed help. It was a miracle there were no deaths or serious injuries.

Across the river, a dozen or more houses were burned to the ground. There were only three houses left on our side—ours and two more. Harrison Watson's belongings had burned in the middle of the river, where he had put them for safekeeping. Flying debris had set them on fire. His house stood untouched on the other side of the river.

People came back on the train to see what was left of their homes. They rummaged through the ashes, hoping some of their life's treasures had been spared. Nothing was left once the fire touched the highly flammable houses of tar paper and dried lumber. It was like touching a match to a haystack.

Everywhere we looked was desolate. Charred snags stood where tall, green trees grew yesterday. The forest floor was bare and ash-covered. Ferns, wildflowers, and velvety moss were no more. There wasn't a bird to be seen or heard. We'd saved our home, but now it stood in a barren wasteland. I'd never seen such ugliness where beauty had reigned. Thunderstorms moved up the mountain and put out the smoldering embers. Dirt and debris washed down the slopes into the river, turning it into a muddy, sluggish stream. Rainbow and speckled trout washed up on the banks, smothered by ashes and mud. Nature would reclaim the mountains, but not for a long time.

For the first time, I thought of Muncie. I couldn't remember when I saw him last. We were so busy thinking of ourselves and our belongings, we forgot to find him. He didn't answer my call, but, hopefully, he'd come back when everything was quiet again. Trout were not the only things to wash up on the river bank. Ma saw Muncie clinging to a log, moving slowly downstream. When she got to him, he was near death and did die later as she pulled him on the bank. It was the last straw—the one that broke the camel's back. My tears came then and helped wash away part of the horror of the last few days.

The company was trying to find jobs for all the Higdon crew. Pa and Ma decided they'd had enough years scared out of them by the fire. They were going out of the mountains to farm again.

Uncle Dave Watson sent word to Pa the J. D. Williams farm was for sale on Upper Middle Creek not far from the place we lived when we came to Tennessee. Pa and Fred went to look it over and liked what they saw. The price was eight hundred dollars for about seventy acres of mostly hilly land.

In the four years since we'd been gone from Oldham's Creek to work in the mountains, Pa and Ma had managed to save seven hundred dollars. He paid that much on the farm, with the promise to pay the other hundred within the coming year.

It was near time for my baby to be born. Ma waited with Wilma and me in the strange quiet of the burned-out camp. The train made daily trips to check on us and a few families on the other end of Higdon.

Friday morning, June 22, Ma sent word to Elkmont for Dr. Montgomery to come and assist with the birth. This was more difficult than my first one. The terror I had lived through took its toll on my health. Before, I had not been frightened, but now every nerve in my body was in knots. Dr. Montgomery gave me nothing to ease my pain. After what seemed an eternity, my baby came—

blue, and unwilling or unable to breathe. Ma and Dr. Montgomery pinched his nose and blew into his mouth, trying to inflate his lungs. Nothing happened. Ma told Fred, who had just arrived from Middle Creek, to get a pan of spring water and hurry. She took Paul by his heels and, holding his head in the other hand, dunked him in the icy water. I heard him suck in air. He cried for two hours without stopping. He wouldn't nurse, he wouldn't be comforted, he just screamed his objection to being brought into this world at all. We could have done quite well without the doctor. Ma had practically handled the delivery alone. She knew how to save the baby's life, at least.

Pa and Ma moved to their new home on Middle Creek near the Williamsburg school. As soon as I was able to travel, we were going with them. The fire had given us reason to go out and try our hand at something else. The company train came to Higdon and we loaded everything on the flatcars to be taken to Elkmont, where it would be picked up by wagons for the journey back to Middle Creek. Almost six years before, we had made this same trip going into the mountains. Life takes unexpected turns. I never thought I'd be returning to the rounded hills of Oldham's Creek and Middle Creek.

IV

1917–1924

We left the camp in September 1917. Nothing had grown back after the fire. When we left, I looked back and tried to remember how it had been when we first came. Near Elkmont, the leaves were beginning to turn into fall finery. These mountains were beautiful. Sadness filled my heart, thinking I would never live here again. This was not a good time to move to a farm. We had no provisions stored away for winter. If Ma and I canned anything, we'd have to buy it. Money was very scarce, since neither Pa nor Fred had worked since the fire four months ago. Pa had used most of his savings to buy the farm. It would be too late to plant anything now except fall turnips.

All these thoughts filled my head as the wagon jolted and swayed along the road. This time, we had no open surrey to ride in. Some of the roads were nothing more than trails. The children were fretful and unhappy. We took turns holding them to cushion them against the painfully bumpy movements of the wagon.

The sun had set and dark shadows fell across the road. Up ahead, on the right, a tidy, gray house stood between an apple orchard and a giant white oak tree near the road. In the back and around the sides, the farm was surrounded with the familiar round hills.

Pa and Fred rented and ran Bob Watson's grist mill on the hill across from Oldham's Creek School. We had very little money left. Ma and I canned and preserved as much as we could. Granny Jane Watson gave us apples and potatoes from their farm. Fred took a wagon to the market in Sevierville to buy what vegetables were left this late in the season.

The cold, damp fall was already taking its toll on the people. Croup was raging all through the valley. Sam and Elgie Maples,

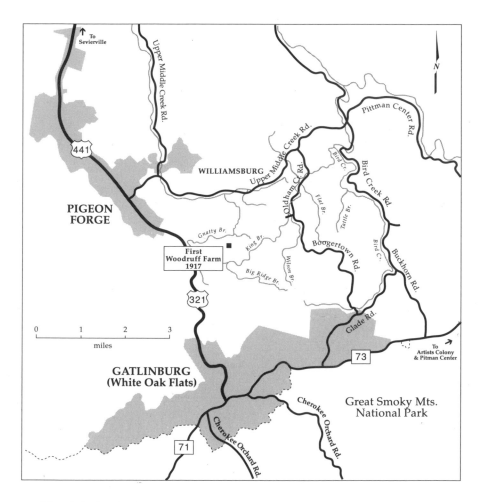

Map 6. Sevier County. After the Higdon Camp fire, Dorie's family moved to the newly acquired farm. When it failed to support the family, they worked for a brief period in the cotton mills in Gaston County, North Carolina.

Dorie: Woman of the Mountains

our nearest neighbors, lost a little girl to the croup. It was called "membranous croup"—a deadly, dreaded part of winter. Fred hitched the horses, Molly and Bess, to the wagon and went to Sevierville to get a casket for her burial. It took him all day in the bad weather. I saw him coming up the road with the draped casket in the back of the wagon. The lump in my throat was unbearable. That box could easily have been for one of my children. We had no defense against this killer of babies.

Already, Wilma had symptoms of it. A hoarse cough in the daytime turned into raspy, hard breathing when the night came. Her lungs filled with heavy mucous, making breathing almost impossible. Ma and I sat up with her and held her upright, hoping to make her breathing easier.

Night is an eternity when a child is sick. Darkness fills the house and your soul. The kerosene lamp on the table made moving, ghostlike shadows on the walls. Everything on earth is shut out except the small, shadowy room and the thing that is choking the life out of your baby.

Her breathing was becoming more difficult. We greased her chest and gave her a tablespoon of sugar wet with three drops of kerosene. Usually, by the time it was all taken, phlegm had broken loose in the lungs. Ma went to the kitchen to slice onions into a skillet of grease to make a poultice for her chest.

The struggle for every breath was wearing her out. She lay limp and lifeless in my lap. A gurgling noise and the coarse cough sent chills through me. Ma grabbed her from me and turned her upside down—hitting her on the back between the shoulder blades. Ma ran her finger into Wilma's mouth and brought out the plug of heavy mucous that was choking her to death. Fear and exhaustion had taken all my strength. My arms and legs felt heavy and immovable.

Wilma was better the next morning. Croup is always better in the morning, giving false hope, but it gets worse as the day wears on. By evening it would try again to take her life. The mailman brought word that another two-year-old girl, just across the hill, had died during the night. He said they were burying her in a homemade casket up on the hillside.

Pa and Ma went to the Maples home to pay their respects. Ma said the little girl was the most beautiful child she'd ever seen. As was the mountain custom, neighbors washed and dressed the body of the dead and did what they could for the family. No funeral home was involved. It was neighbor caring for neighbor in times of sorrow.

To make matters worse, rumors of a killer flu began coming into Middle Creek. Some called it Spanish Flu and said it was caused by chemicals being used in the war in Europe. People were dying all over the country. Nobody was safe. We thought it was carried by the winds into every valley and cove. Sevierville was reporting more and more deaths from this strange disease. We were afraid, but we didn't know what we could do to protect ourselves. Ma thought sulphur would protect us, so we each took a teaspoonful every night. We lived in terror as people all around us died. Granny Watson's stepdaughter died. Dr. Ben Cogdill died. Pa's niece, Ethel Mills, died. Many others had it and recovered.

Luther did a lot of outside work for the neighbors who were sick. He fed and cared for their livestock, cut firewood, and took food that Ma, Lola, and I had prepared for people who couldn't help themselves. He never went inside their homes, thinking he'd have less exposure to the flu if he stayed outside. We all escaped by the grace of God, and maybe the sulphur helped, too. Many kinds of preventive medicine were practiced by different people. Fred's sisters in North Carolina, Blanche and Grace, cared for the sick and then went home and ate a plateful of fried onions to ward off the flu. Although exposed to it many times, they remained well.

Winter passed slowly and agonizingly. Ma and I didn't always agree. She had her own way of doing things and wanted no suggestions from me. After living in my own home and caring for my family in my way, it wasn't easy to be treated as a child again by Ma. She was very much in command of her home, as she should be.

In all human hearts is the notion that things will be better when spring comes. I watched, longingly, for the first signs—a flower, a bird, a warm breeze, anything to give me hope and courage. And it came as always, on its own terms. The feelings of despair and emptiness slowly faded as I took my babies on long walks through the hillsides. The apple orchard brought back memories of a nine-year-old who played house and dreamed dreams not many years ago.

We all worked at getting the garden and corn crop in the ground. The farm had poor soil, used up generations ago and never replenished. It was doubtful we would grow enough for our own use, certainly none to sell. The tobacco crop would probably bring in the only cash we could make from the farm. Pa always looked up at the sky in the morning for a weather sign. He said Matthew 16:2–3 told him how to predict the weather. "...When it is evening, ye say, It will be fair weather: for the sky is red. And in the morning, It will be foul weather today: for the sky is red. ...."

We started going to Oldham's Creek Church again. Most of my cousins were there with their new families. It was good to get to know them and be around people our own age. When the spring revival started, Ma kept Wilma and Paul while we (Luke, Lola, Fred, and I) went to church. We joined in singing the joyous hymns and were caught up in the message of salvation and love being preached. The first night's altar call brought many from their seats to the mourner's bench in the front row. Touched, but not willing to go forward, Fred and I rode home in thoughtful silence. The soft rhythm of the horses' hooves and the call of a distant whippoorwill were the only sounds on the road.

We were torn with indecision the next night. The need to go and hear the message again overcame our excuses for not going. When the altar call came, we went hand-in-hand to the front and sat on the mourner's bench while the preacher and deacons prayed for us and our salvation. We would be baptized as an outward symbol of our acceptance of Christ and our new life in Him.

Determined not to be "trunk Baptists," we joined the church

Lola, Ma, and Dorie (*left to right*) wear their Sunday-best dresses with lace, and their jewelry.

and went every Sunday we could. In the summer we had "all-day singing and dinner on the ground." We'd get up early, kill and fry a chicken, take Saturday's cake, and have a good time.

Folks who didn't always come to church showed up for the "harp singing." Anyone who wanted to lead was welcome to try. One elderly gentleman hobbled down the aisle, stooped over and using two canes—one in each hand—to claim his turn to lead. We all wondered how such a feeble man could stand up long enough to lead. In a moment, he was transformed. Dropping both canes, his back became arrow straight, he lifted both arms and began. Song after song was flawlessly directed. When he was finished, he picked up both canes, his back bowed low, and he hobbled back up the aisle.

Decoration day was a festive but sad occasion, usually held in June. People we hadn't seen since last year's decoration would be there. In a way, it was a family reunion. The day before the decoration, men would gather and clean off the cemetery so clean that not a blade of grass was left. Fresh dirt was heaped on the graves, making them look bare and new. Resolve and acceptance of past grief were hard to hold onto when we stood by the newly shaped and bare graves of loved ones long gone from us. It was as if the years had dissolved and we were back at the time of our bereavement when our family and friends had just died. Some wept as they placed their floral offerings on the graves.

Everyone brought flowers, sometimes in containers, but mostly just handfuls of half-wilted blossoms to lay lovingly on the grave of a relative or friend. Wild roses grew in profusion along the roads. Unless women had flowers around the house, they brought roses. Ma had lilies and dahlias in the yard. She never lived anywhere without taking her dahlia bulbs. They were pretty to look at, but they outdid the skunk for odor. The big, saucer-sized blooms made the plants bow low to the ground. I never understood why Ma liked them so much.

In the fall of 1919, Pa brought word that Uncle Dave Watson was dead. I felt a great loss. Uncle Dave was a strict disciplinarian, but he had been good to me. When I stayed with them, he expected the same obedience from me as he did from his own children. I could almost hear him say, "The ramps are up," just like he did when he first brought us to Tennessee. He was buried in Boogertown, but I didn't go to the funeral. Our third child was due any day now, and a ride in a jolting wagon might cause me to give birth in the open road, Indian style.

Since the baby was due, Dr. John Ogle made regular visits to check on me. On January 21, he came by soon after my labor started. He gave me some new medicine to speed up my labor. It had the opposite effect—everything stopped. He said there was no use leaving, because he'd just have to come back in the middle of the night. About three in the morning, on January 22, our daughter, Mary Edith, was born. She was a tiny, wrinkled little thing, the smallest of my babies. There was no crying with this one. She was happy and contented with her lot in life. Hungry for nourishment and love, she nestled contentedly into my breast.

The farm and the grist mill weren't making enough money for two families to live on, and, besides, Fred and Ma were increasingly at odds over how to bring up children. We had many long talks about what we should do—go back to the Little River Lumber Company or try something new. Nightmares about the Higdon fire were still too real, and I was afraid to go back to the mountains with my babies.

While we were waiting to decide our course for the future, a ghost story involving one of the more prominent members of the community was the most talked-about news. It seems Henry was walking alone on Gnatty Branch Road when he saw a woman coming toward him from the other direction. The only thing he noticed about her at first was her shiny, emerald-green dress. It must have been satin, because it reflected the sunlight as she came closer. He saw her raise her hand in greeting, but, at the same time, he noticed something else—she had no head!

He didn't run back down the road the way he'd come, he jumped the ditch and climbed and clawed his way up the side of a steep hill. His aunt, who was our neighbor, said he was incoherent when he got to her house. He got into bed but couldn't stop shaking. She called the doctor to come and see if he'd lost his mind. The doctor said he was the most frightened man he'd ever seen and gave him something to help him sleep. His aunt said he wasn't drinking "spirits" and was of sound mind.

The emerald lady of Gnatty Branch was not seen again, so

far as I know. Henry could have been the victim of a practical joke. The only thing that makes the story believable is that nobody in this area could have afforded an emerald-green satin dress!

The time had come to eat my words, after vowing never to go to North Carolina, it seemed to be the only solution to our problem. In 1922, Fred went to Gaston County, North Carolina, to see about work in a new cotton mill across the river from his family. The Copes lived on a farm and worked in the mill. They wrote glowing reports of a land "flowing with milk and honey." Such reports couldn't go unheeded. We were going to earn our share of the riches.

S. W. and C. B. Cramer founded the Cramerton Mills in 1921. As in the tradition of cotton-mill owners, the Cramers acted as benevolent parents to their workers. A village bearing their name grew up around the mills.

Fred was hired as a supervisor and would be paid $8.50 a day. He came back to Middle Creek to move us. We took our dishes, linens, two beds, a dresser, and a cookstove. Having lived in the Little River Lumber Company partially furnished house, we had little furniture of our own.

Warm June weather made the trip a joy. After many uneventful months on Middle Creek, the thoughts of starting a new life was exciting. Eight dollars and fifty cents a day would buy a lot of things, and I'd be in charge of my own home again.

Fred's family met us at the depot with a wagon. All his brothers helped load our boxes and barrels and took us to their home. We would spend the night with them and move in the morning. They hadn't seen our last two babies. It had been several years since our last visit, when we lived at Three Forks.

The company house was big and beautiful compared to other places we'd lived. It had two big bedrooms, a kitchen with an icebox, hot and cold running water, and indoor plumbing. Almost everything we needed was in the village. The streets had gaslights, medical attention was available, and a motion-picture theater added to the excitement of the place.

These company houses were provided by the Cramerton cotton mills in North Carolina. Fred and Dorie lived in a house on the left side of the picture.

Fred's family were frequent visitors, happy to have him near them again. I still didn't feel comfortable around them. Maybe it was my own fault that we didn't understand each other better. I was always quiet and reserved, in complete contrast to their boisterous, laughing manner. Mountain people didn't say anything if they were not sure what to say. So, usually, I said nothing. I always remembered a quote from Abraham Lincoln who said, "It's better to keep your mouth shut and let people wonder if you're a fool than to speak and prove you are."

Fred's brother, Harry, was a wild, fun-loving extrovert. After being out at night, and not wanting to let his mother know the late hours he kept, he'd sneak in our back bedroom window and sleep on a pallet on the floor. When we got out of bed in the morning, one of us was sure to stumble over Harry's sleeping form. His tall tales could make Paul Bunyon, the giant of the north woods, seem like a dwarf.

We went to church with the Copes. They were Methodist. Grandfathers on both sides of the family had been Methodist ministers and several uncles were church stewards. To please them, we became members of their church. I really didn't see that much difference between the Baptists and Methodists, but, still, I wondered what Ma would say when she heard.

Back home in Middle Creek, Lola had married Am Townsend and given birth to her first child. The baby was stillborn and Lola was very sick. Ma wrote and told us to come home if we wanted to see her again. By the time we got home, she'd improved and was recovering with the help of Dr. John Ogle.

It was good to be with my family again. We described Cramerton as a wonderland, so Pa and Ma decided to go back with us and work in the mills. Pa hadn't been able to break even on the farm. They would live with us, and we would share expenses. That way, we hoped to be able to save some of our money. Luther didn't want to go with us. There were several girls in Boogertown who had caught his eye, especially a little, red-haired Watson girl. He stayed with Lola and Am on the farm.

Although Pa and Fred were making good wages, we couldn't get fresh milk for the children. The company store didn't sell it. Once a week, a local farmer came through the village selling milk, butter, and eggs. We bought all we could store in the icebox, but it was never enough. The icebox didn't keep food as fresh and cold as our springhouse in the mountains. Edith, who'd just been weaned, sat at the table and cried when we had no milk. She grew thin and pale and was much too small for her age.

Once a week, a butcher came with a wagon full of fresh beef. We had many delicious roasts and stews. Beef was a luxury few mountain people could afford. It was more profitable to sell any calf we didn't need. Rarely was a steer slaughtered for food. So we enjoyed the chance to have all the beef we wanted. Suddenly, the

Dorie's sister, Lola, *left*, and their cousin Ruth Watson pose on their wedding day. They were married in a double ceremony. Dorie made both dresses.

butcher stopped coming to town. Fred heard that he had been arrested for selling horse and donkey meat as beef. He had made his supply of beef go further by adding horse meat to the pile. Had we eaten horse meat, or were we always lucky enough to get the beef? I'd like to think that luck was with us.

Ma and I were getting along all right. This time, we were living in my house, and I felt secure enough to do what I wanted. Still, we didn't always agree about the children. Over my objections, Ma had been giving Paul coffee to drink. He had always been high-strung and temperamental, and I thought the coffee added to his problem. Every morning she'd pour coffee in a saucer to cool and let him drink it.

His love for coffee led us to a near-tragedy that could have cost him his life or his leg. He pulled a chair up to the stove and turned the coffeepot over on himself. The steaming brown coffee poured on his leg and filled his shoe. He stood screaming, unable to move. When I got to him I thought his pants had kept him from being badly burned. I jerked them off and saw the stocking was steaming, too. When I pulled the top of his stocking away from his leg, the skin came off in thin, white strips. He was burned from his knee to his ankle. The skin kept the imprint of the knitted stripes in the stocking.

The company doctor came and coated the burn with paraffin. He had been a Navy doctor before coming to Cramerton. His methods of practice were new to me. Everytime a scab formed on the burn, he'd pull it off with tweezers. Paul's temperature was high, he cried constantly and couldn't sleep. This went on for weeks until the doctor said Paul wouldn't get well, but we could see another doctor if we wanted to. He didn't come back anymore. I was relieved to see the last of him. As soon as he left, I washed Paul's leg in warm, soapy water and sprinkled it every few hours with talcum powder. A scab began to form, and his fever went down.

We wouldn't let him walk, and it was everybody's job to entertain him. Fred bought a little red wagon so we could pull him instead of having to carry him. After weeks of pampering, he didn't want to walk on his own. We had to start at the beginning and teach him again.

Rumors began circulating that the mill would close. There were over a hundred textile mills operating in Gaston County at that time. Outside influences caused a breakdown of communications between the mill owners and the mill workers. Organizers of the textile union came with literature and unasked-for advice, telling the workers how bad off they were. We were doing well. Pa and Fred had managed to save some money.

About this time, Communist activist Fred Beal and George Pershing of the Communist party paper, *The Daily Worker*, started making heated, inflammatory speeches to the workers. The Communist party saw the cotton mills as the lifeline to the South. If they could control the textile workers, the South would be theirs. After frenzied meetings, violent strikes erupted all over the county. The National Guard was called out to keep order. Sensing the coming battles with the unions and the postwar recession, the Cramerton Mill closed.

Panic swept through the town. What would we do, and where would we go? Mr. Cope and three of his sons worked at the mill. Never ones to work with the soil, complete dependence on farming was out of the question. Pa said we could come back to Middle Creek and survive, at least.

Mr. Cope was interested in some new industry in New Hampshire. Always one to chase butterflies and rainbows, he wanted to go and see if there was money to be made. The boys gave him enough money to go scouting for the pot of gold. When he got there, he found winter so severe and the ground frozen so deep, the people couldn't bury their dead until the spring thaw. The milder winters of North Carolina hadn't prepared him for the Arctic-like cold of New Hampshire.

Pa and Ma had gone back to Tennessee, Fred and I were waiting for a report from Mr. Cope. I was relieved—no, I was eternally thankful that the report was bad and we could go home to Middle Creek. We were going home. The mountains might seem hostile to some people, but they were a shelter and a blessing for me. I lived in their shadows. As they gave strength to my ancestors long ago, they gave strength to me now.

We came back to the farm on Middle Creek. The small frame house stood in the valley completely surrounded by the same smooth hills which ran from Oldham's Creek to the Glades. A small stream ran through the meadow not far from the front porch. Peach and apple trees covered the hillside opposite the road on the right. The huge white oak tree stood in the clearing between the house and road. The oak was so large and old, it must have been there hundreds of years. The children had forgotten they'd ever lived here.

At least this time we were not penniless. We had saved some money, and Pa and Ma had been able to keep most of theirs. Ma heard that a phone line had been put up through our part of the county. She put in her order for a phone and waited. Soon we had a new telephone attached to the wall. All we had to do was lift the receiver and turn the crank to talk to almost anybody in Boogertown and Middle Creek.

Am, Lola, and Luther had gone back to the lumbering job in the mountains. Am operated an "incline skidder" that brought logs down steep mountains by using guy wires and leverage cables. He and Ben Wilson were the company experts in this operation. The pay was good, and he soon bought a new T-Model Ford car. Luther learned to drive it before Am did and became the family chauffeur.

Luther had ulterior motives. He was courting the red-headed schoolteacher from Boogertown and needed a car to get to her house on the weekends. On the 26th of July 1924, Pa co-signed a note at the bank of Sevierville for $223. Luther was buying a Chevrolet Touring Car from the Watson Motor Company. He paid $25 a month until the debt was paid off. He married Willie Watson before many months passed. She gave up her career as a teacher and came to live in the mountains for the first time.

Fred and Pa showed no interest in the car and still went by Shank's Mare (walking) or in the jolt wagon. There were two work horses on the farm, but they never rode them anywhere.

This would be Wilma's first year in school. Audrey Ownby was the teacher in the one-room Williamsburg school on Middle Creek Road. Ma wanted to make her a pretty lunch basket so she wouldn't have to carry a tin bucket. She sent for a package of red dye. After peeling the bark from willow branches, she dyed them brilliant red and made them into a basket with a top. The red basket caught the eye of several people, and Wilma had a hard time keeping it.

Her Cousin Kate was the same age as Wilma. They played together but fought constantly. They'd play quietly and then, without warning, turn on each other and fight like wildcats. The red basket added a new hitch to their relationship. Kate wanted it and was determined to have it, while Wilma was equally determined to keep it. To stop the fighting, I finally stopped packing her lunch in it and gave her a tin bucket like everybody else carried. The basket sat under her bed, filled with dried flowers and shiny rocks plucked from the creek.

Our second son, Charles Edward, was born December 29, 1922. Dr. John Ogle came to deliver him. He thought it was a false alarm, and, remembering he had spent the night waiting for Edith to arrive, he went over the hill to visit his mother, Martha Jane Ogle. Her farm was the next one over from Pa's.

Mrs. Ogle had been married to Ma's uncle, Samuel Maples. They had two children, Westly and Lucinda. Cindy died when she was young. According to family lore, Uncle Sam had been killed while he was working in his cornfield. Some say he was shot in the back by snipers who thought he had caused their still to be discovered and destroyed. After he died, Aunt Martha married Isaac Ogle. They had five children, two sons and three daughters. Both of their sons were doctors—Dr. John Ogle and Dr. Ashley Ogle. Although not really related, we shared some relatives with Dr. John Ogle and felt he was part of the family.

Minutes after he left, Charles decided it was time to make his entrance into the world. Ma called the Ogles to have the doctor return. By the time he came back, Charles had already been born. "Dorie," he said, "I think you do this deliberately. I can't tell when you're ready nor how long it will take. Try to be on time the next time, young lady."

"I hope there won't be a next time," Ma said. She let me know she thought my family was big enough now and I should stop with this baby—my fourth. I didn't know how I would accomplish this without leaving Fred. Mountain women thought you couldn't become pregnant while you had a nursing baby. It seemed to work for me. Probably, I let my children nurse too long just to keep from having another baby so soon. I had been able to keep them three or more years apart. Anyway, it was easy enough for Ma to say, because she never had to worry about the problem since my baby sister died. Because of her injuries during the birth, no more babies were conceived.

We were preoccupied with the new baby while Pa and Fred were trying to make a living any way they could. The farm was worn out and we knew it wouldn't support two families. Besides, Pa wanted to go back to the railroad job in the mountains. He was very good at trestle building, so he got his job back without any trouble. Sam Maples, Ma's cousin, took their furniture to Elkmont to be sent by train to Jake's Creek.

Fred and I stayed on the farm with an almost empty house, since Pa and Ma took most of their belongings with them. Fred did some farming, but most of his time was spent cutting acid wood and tan bark. After he cut a wagonload, it was taken to Pigeon Forge to be sold. We scratched out a living this way for about a year before we went back to logging on Jake's Creek. We hadn't been back to the mountains since the Higdon fire.

V

1924–1937.

Jake's Creek was being logged for the second time. Years before, it had been one of the first places to attract the attention of the lumber company. Pa had helped rebuild the railroad, and there was still evidence that fire had destroyed countless acres of timber. Nature had restored the mountain, and the loggers were ready to strip it again.

Fred went to work on the skidder. Instead of railroad cars, the company had built two-family houses along the railroad. As luck would have it, our companion family was the one who still hadn't forgiven me for accidently pouring hot water on his favorite bear dog when we lived at Three Forks. They were older than we were, so there was not much to talk about anyway. The bear dog had been dead for years, but his ghost still stood between us. I don't know how he died, but it wasn't caused by my accident.

After we'd been there a few weeks, Paul began having headaches and an upset stomach. Fred went by Dr. Montgomery's and asked him to come and check on him. Late in the afternoon, Dr. Montgomery knocked on the door. It had been years since I'd seen him, but he still looked the same. He asked what I had been doing for Paul. "I gave him half of an aspirin," I said.

His face turned the familiar purple-red with rage. Something akin to the voice of Thor rang through the little house. "God-All-Mighty, woman, you're going to kill him. Throw those things away!" Dr. Montgomery was a strong believer in the curative powers of calomel, castor oil, and iodine. Of course, if you were possessed by evil spirits, his bedside manner would scare the devil out of you!

Dr. Montgomery was not a man to annoy. He had the personal-

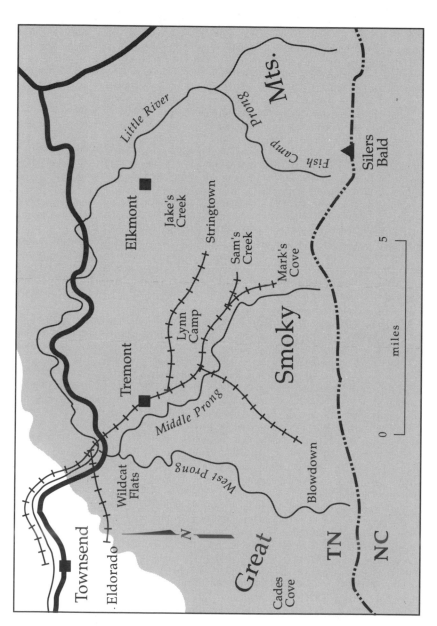

Map 7. Home and work in the Smokies. Between 1924 and 1937, most of Dorie's family worked for the Little River Lumber Company in its final years.

ity of a Smoky Mountain black bear. In other words, he had no patience with his patients. Three hung-over loggers showed up at his Elkmont office complaining of being sick, but denying the cause. He gave them large spoonfuls of croton oil. Croton oil is a heavy, bitter purgative many times more potent than castor oil, given routinely in the spring to rid the body of the impurities of winter living. Fred said the three showed up for work about a week later—a little wiser, a little thinner, and a little quieter.

The good doctor was said to be seen throwing quilts out the front door of a house where his patient had pneumonia. The poor man was burning up with fever, and his worried, well-meaning wife was trying to keep him warm and help him get well. Dr. Montgomery grabbed the cover and threw it out, while berating the wife for trying to kill her husband with kindness. "He needs to be soaked in cold river water to bring down the blankety-blank fever," he shouted.

Soon after, Uncle Jimmy Maples was very sick and in great pain. Dr. Montgomery came and examined him. Appendicitis was his diagnosis. He sent a message to Jefferson City for a surgeon to come and operate. It was two or three days before the surgeon came. Uncle Jimmy's fever was so high, cold water was brought from the river to bathe him. He couldn't stand anything to touch him. Ma made a tent out of the bed cover by lining chairs beside the bed and draping the cover over them.

When the surgeon came, they cleaned off the kitchen table and operated on him. By now, his fever and the infection were too severe for him to survive. As a gesture of friendship, one of our neighbors came to shave Uncle Jimmy before he died. Mr. Wilson cut his own finger on the straight razor and, without thinking, used this finger to clean a little nick he'd made on Uncle Jimmy's chin. Mr. Wilson became ill several days later. Dr. Montgomery thought he had blood poisoning and it had come from the infection in Uncle Jimmy's body.

Four days after the surgery, Uncle Jimmy died. A casket was brought up from Elkmont on a flatcar. They placed his body in the casket and sent it out on the same car to take it back to Elkmont, where it would be taken by wagon to the family cemetery in Boogertown. We didn't go to his funeral because it took all day to get there and another to get back.

In 1924, work was going well when "Fire on the mountain!" echoed through the camp. The fire stayed high on the mountain during the night. We stayed up and watched it burn along the ridges. Nobody in camp went to bed. We had to be ready to leave in a moment's notice. By morning we knew it wouldn't come close to the camp, and everybody went back to work. I wouldn't have stayed and fought this one. At the first suggestion, I would have been on the train, going away from the terror.

Tom and Martha Moore were the best friends and neighbors we could have. Mrs. Moore loved my children as her own and had them in and out of her house. We didn't have a cow, so she shared her milk and butter with us. She made loaves of delicious light bread with yeast. When the wind brought wisps of the nutty, light odor of baking bread into the windows, we were happy because Mrs. Moore would soon be knocking on our door with a warm loaf of bread and a dish of golden, yellow butter to melt on the delicate, white slices. No cake ever tasted better.

Wilma and Paul walked to a one-room school not far from home, near Elkmont. Older boys in camp were a constant source of trouble. Teachers came and went quickly. Paul had so many teachers and so little attention, he memorized the primer from hearing other children read it. He couldn't read a word but could recite it so perfectly they didn't know the difference. It took them awhile to figure out how he could read that book so well but couldn't read or spell anything else.

In the summer, Dr. Montgomery sent word to all the families to come and get typhoid shots. I'm not sure if the state was giving them free or if the company was paying for them. We rode the flatcar to Elkmont, hot cinders peppering our faces and hair as the train puffed along. At the edge of the ballfield, near the doctor's office, Edith stepped on a yellowjackets' nest. They swarmed all over her. She screamed and jumped up and down, unable to step off the nest. She had a dozen or more stings before we could get her away from it. Dr. Montgomery put wet baking soda on the welts. By the time we got home, she had a fever and couldn't walk. As always, Ma didn't approve of the doctor's treatment. She said we should use tobacco juice or mud. I compromised. I soaked Pa's chewing tobacco in water and mixed it with baking soda. By morning she was better, and the big red welts were gone.

Winter came early that year. We had snow on the ground for four straight months. We had preserved some food to help out when Fred couldn't work because of the weather. We wrapped our plumpest tomatoes individually in pages torn from the Sears catalog and stored them under the bed. We kept apples the same way. The apples had been given to us because Paul used his best manners. Mr. Sam Cook had a beautiful apple orchard between the camp and the school. Children, on their way to school, shook the trees and helped themselves to the apples. Naturally, Mr. Cook wasn't fond of children during apple time.

He was picking apples one afternoon just as the children went past. When they saw him, they scattered. Paul stopped to watch him, not saying anything. Mr. Cook noticed him and asked what he wanted. Paul said he told him, "Nothing, Sir. It's just that you have the prettiest and best apples I ever saw." After that, he walked away. Later that night, Mr. Cook brought a box of apples and set them on the porch. He told Fred they were for that nice boy of ours.

It was here Fred became a hunter, not so much by choice but by necessity. Money was scarce, and, because of that, so was meat. We ate squirrel meat but still no rabbit because we were afraid of rabbit fever. We ate the squirrel fried crispy and brown like chicken or boiled with dumplings. Trout was plentiful, but, somehow, we never thought about fish being meat. Fish was just fish. Meat came from furry creatures.

In 1926 our job at Jake's Creek was finished. Our house was

lifted onto a flatcar and moved to Wildcat flats, just below Tremont. Fred was supervisor on the skidder now. Aunt Rintha and family were already on the job. Paul and Wilma could walk to the school in Tremont.

The mountains were beautiful. Cold, crystal springs cascaded down the slopes. We got our water from one several yards away from the house. Countless trips were made to it everyday. One evening at dusk, Wilma took a bucket and started for water. Unknown to her, the water had attracted something else, too. Just above the spring, two golden eyes glared at her, watching every move. A wildcat crouched low to the ground, ready to spring when she came close enough. Wilma could feel the intensity of the gaze before she saw the cat. She froze for a second as the golden eyes narrowed. She dropped the bucket and ran toward the house. She didn't look back to see if the cat was coming. Here eyes were on the crossties. If she missed one and fell, the cat would be on her in a minute. The door flew open and a white-faced ghost of a child collapsed on the floor. Fred took his rifle and went back to the spring, but the cat was gone.

Wilma and Aunt Rintha's daughter, Kate, were like wild Indians. They had learned to play together without fighting. When we lived on Middle Creek they were alternately friends and enemies. Here they worked as a team at making mischief. Wilma kept coming home with scrapes and bruises all over.

"Wilma, what have you been doing, wrestling a wildcat?"

"No, Momma (I wouldn't let her call me Ma), Kate and I have been swinging on a grapevine and trying to land on top of a big stump. Sometimes we miss."

They caught snakes and spring lizards without a hint of fear. Anybody who showed the slightest alarm at their pets became a target for devilment. One friend had the normal, girlish horror of creepy, crawly things and was a marked victim. She kept her distance and posted lookouts, but she couldn't escape. I never knew which girl put the snake on her, but they both paid the same price for doing it.

One of the rare treats for everyone was a new shipment of bologna sausage at the company store. It tasted like manna from heaven after a steady diet of ham, bacon, salt pork, dried pork, boiled pork, and fried pork. One old mountaineer was first in line when the sausage was cut. "My Caldonia (his wife) sure loves that salonie sausage," he'd say through a toothless smile. So, bologna sausage became "salonie sausage" ever after.

This winter, Fred and his crew were logging high on the mountain. He left at dawn and returned at dusk. His lunch was packed in a tin bucket. Loggers never took anything to drink from home. Crystal springs were everywhere, and they drank from them. Somewhere on the mountain, Fred drank from a contaminated spring. He complained of weakness and nausea but kept working. One morning he got up and tried to get dressed for work. When he got to the door, he fell to the floor unconscious. I thought he was dead. The children were still in bed. Hearing my frantic efforts to wake him, they stood behind me, white-faced with fear. With their help, we lifted him to the bed. He was burning up with fever.

We would have to get word to Dr. Montgomery in Elkmont that he was needed. When the first train went out, our message was relayed to him. It was noon before he came. Fred was in and out of consciousness. The doctor was furious! In one of Fred's lucid moments, the doctor admonished him, "You've got typhoid fever. Why didn't you call me sooner? You could spread it through these mountains." "I didn't want to get into a hole (financially)," Fred said feebly. The company paid you when you worked, with no time off for illness or anything else. Dr. Montgomery bellowed, "That's a good way to get into a six-foot hole for keeps."

He gave me instructions on caring for Fred; castor oil with a few drops of turpentine, buttermilk to drink, and that was all. Wilma, Paul, and Edith were sent to Ma's. I'd need all my time and energy to take care of their father. Charles was so small, I didn't want him away from me. He played quietly or sat in my lap while we waited for Fred to get well.

For days, Fred talked and moaned but never remembered

doing it. He perspired so much that I changed his clothing and bedding several times a day. When he started feeling better, he begged for something to eat, especially cornbread. I didn't trust him alone with food. When I went out to milk, I'd hide every bit, every crumb. He was not to have anything solid for two weeks, then he could only have baked apples.

People usually think of typhoid as a summer sickness, but it knows no season. Fred was sick in December. He was off from work two months. His clothes hung loosely from his bony frame, and his head looked too big for his body.

Our children had their first big Christmas while they were at Ma's. The lumber company had a party for all the students in the Tremont School. We didn't have Christmas at home. The children hung up their stockings for candy or an apple but no toys. We never had a Christmas tree. Mrs. Townsend, wife of the company owner, sent toys for all the children in school. Back in November, they had made a list of the three things they wanted most. Mrs. Townsend selected one item on every list and sent it to the school. At the Christmas party, the gifts were given out, beautifully wrapped with the child's name on the appropriate one. My children saw their first Christmas tree there.

The building at Tremont was an all-purpose building. It was the church, school, and later the theater where movies were shown. D. L. Tipton said it was used for salvation, education, hellfire, and damnation. Some folks thought the movies were works of the devil. Part of our heritage was a large puritanical streak handed down through the ages.

The church was nondenominational. Colonel Townsend made sure a Methodist minister was there at least once a month. Otherwise, anybody could preach if he had a congregation. Appalachian people were not "joiners." They felt they were preaching the Word of God. They didn't feel it necessary to designate a four-walled structure and paint a label over the door before they could practice their religious beliefs. Basic Christian beliefs were held dear. The denomination idea made no sense to them.

The Tremont Community Center was all things to all people. It was the church, school, theater, and wrestling arena for Saturday night matches brought in from the outside. Ladies were welcome to come, if they dared. Dorie and her family lived in a portable housing unit behind this building and on the right.

All kinds of religious beliefs were brought in as people came from the outside to work in the lumbering business. Without my knowledge, my children would slip away and go eavesdrop outside the building when the Holiness had their services. The Holiness were the most vocal and active. When they all started shouting and moving, the children watched through the windows. One large lady was known for her joyous elation when the spirit overtook her. At one meeting, she was shouting and jumping for joy, when the elastic in her panties broke. The white garment fell around her ankles. She just stepped out of them and said, "Praise the Lord. It's all right anyhow!"

That phrase brought the end of my children's unauthorized visits to the services. When they first started applying it to every mistake they made, I wondered where they heard it. After much discussion, they told me what they had done. We had a serious talk on the rights of others to practice religion as they saw fit without critical observations from peeping toms.

There were folk who were Methodist, Holiness, Missionary Baptist, Primitive Baptist, footwashing Baptist, a sprinkling of Presbyterians, and a few Campbellites. The footwashing Baptists held much fascination for the mountain youth. One young man in camp fell in love with a pretty girl from Cades Cove who happened to belong to this particular group. He was so much in love, he agreed to go with her to church. For a long time, he escaped the foot bath ritual, but his time was coming. He promised this Sunday for sure. He lived in a boardinghouse with several men who wouldn't take his sudden interest in religion seriously. Saturday night, he bathed and laid out his clothes for his big Sunday. During the night, some of his friends took his socks and poured soot into them, folded them neatly, and put them back with his clothing.

He was up and dressed early. His friends followed at a distance as he made his way to the church. The service went well, and the footwashing was about to begin. All the men sat in chairs at the front of the church. A large pan of water sat at their feet. It was a sign of humility and love to wash the feet of another. Each man was seated, put his feet into the water and another man washed and dried them. When the young swain's time came, he sat down and peeled off his socks. He held them dangling in his hand while he stared, in horror, at his feet. It looked like he had on another pair of socks. The black soot covered him from ankle to toe. Grabbing his shoes, he bolted to the door in time to see his bunkhouse friends rolling with laughter outside the church. Needless to say, the romance was dead. He'd never be able to face his girl again.

While the mountain folk took their religion seriously, they enjoyed a good joke—so long as it was told on a group other than their own. The Methodists teased the Baptists about feeding their preacher so much fried chicken when he ate with them. They told the story of a good Baptist preacher who dropped his false teeth into the river when he was freshening up before he preached. All the brothers and sisters went to the river to help hunt for the teeth. An old Methodist sitting on the bank watched the frantic search and then said, "Yore wastin' yore time lookin'. Jest git a chicken drumstick, tie a string around it and drap hit in the water. Them teeth'll jest naturally chomp on the drumstick and you kin haul 'em up!"

With so many preachers using the same church, it was difficult for us to know which denomination was visiting us when one came to call. The Baptists tell this one on the Methodists. An old logger was out working in his garden when his son ran up and cried, "Pa, Pa, the preacher's here!" "Which one, son, the Methodist or the Baptist?" "Don't know, Pa," the boy replied. "Well, son, you run back and find out. If it's the Baptist preacher, lock up the chicken house. If it's the Methodist preacher, you climb on your Ma's lap and don't move 'til I get home!"

Presbyterians didn't escape the mountain humor, either. It seems a young Presbyterian missionary came into the mountains to preach to the sinners. He started up the mountains, but night overtook him before he could find shelter. The weather was cold, so he made a bed in the leaves and covered himself with a good, thick layer. The next morning when the sun came up, he saw a cabin on the mountainside. He knocked on the door and called out his greetings. A thin-faced woman opened the door just enough to peek at him.

"Is your husband here?" he asked.

"Nope, my man's gone ahuntin," she said.

"This is the Sabbath," said the missionary. "Isn't he afraid of the Lord?"

"Nope," she retorted, "he ain't afeared of nothin, cause he's got his double-barreled shotgun with him."

Beginning to doubt the wisdom of invading these mountains, the missionary asked, "Please, are there any Presbyterians in these parts?"

"I ain't never heered o' none, but go look on the woodshed out back, he skins every varmint he shoots. You jest might find one's hide tacked to the wall."

"Woman, you are living in darkness," he said.

"Wal, I know that. I been tryin' to git my man to cut a winder in this cabin since we moved in, but he ain't never had the time."

The missionary prayerfully folded his hands and gazed into heaven. "Alas, for the lost sheep of Israel."

"Don't know nuthin about Mr. Israel's sheep, but old man Skinner keeps a flock 'o sheep acrost yan mountain."

Pleadingly he said, "Sister, are you ready for that great day that's coming?"

"Wal," she said, "I don't reckon I'll git to go. I never go nowhere anymore. Would you not tell my man about hit neither? Fer iffen you tell him, he'll go and iffen he does, he'll git drunk."

The poor missionary left, a beaten man. This is probably why you find more Baptists and Methodists in the Smokies than Presbyterians.

For many months, Tremont remained our central location. All our jobs had been within a radius of a few miles. Stringtown was about a mile above Tremont. There were at least five places called Stringtown in the areas between Elkmont and Tremont. The name came from the way the housing was placed beside the railroad going side-by-side up the mountains—like beads on a string. Everyone who lived at "Stringtown" thinks theirs is the only one in the mountains. It is still a source of disagreement between the older ones who remember living in a place called "Stringtown." Our "Stringtown" was on the upper end of Lynn Camp out of Elkmont.

We had to move so much we didn't mind it anymore. Folks loved to tease Henry Ogle, who worked on the railroad with Pa. They said he'd moved so many times his chickens would lie down, cross their legs, and wait for him to tie them with string. His guineas wouldn't go to the river to drink without leaving one posted as a lookout to make sure Henry didn't move without them. If the lookout saw any suspicious movement, he'd call, "Come back, come back." All the guineas came back squawking, ready to move.

It was said that during a revival at Tremont, Henry killed most of his chickens to feed the preacher. One old rooster was left. Every time he saw the preacher come, he'd hide under the house. Every so often, he'd stick his head out and softly crow, "Is he gone yet?" The old guinea would answer, "Go back, go back."

Our cows were usually taken along the trails to the new camp. All the poultry was put into coops or had their feet tied and laid on the flat cars. Everything was left in the house, which was picked up by cranes and lifted on flatcars, too.

Life was good to us now. The children liked school, timber was plentiful, and the weather beautiful. Our nearest neighbors were Mr. and Mrs. Eli Ownby, Aunt Isabell Barns, and Mr. and Mrs. Beecher Townsend. Wilma, Paul, and Edith spent hours playing on the rocks in the river that ran behind our house. It was a crystal playground, usually calm and friendly. However, sometimes without warning, a heavy thunderstorm high on the mountain changed it into a roaring, tearing monster. At night, after a storm, we could hear the giant rocks being pushed and crushed together by its force. Trees, loosened by the flood, crashed into the water to be swept downstream.

Summer storms could be savage and frightening. Winds raged through the mountains flattening strips of timber as they went. We didn't hear the word "tornado," but that must have been what they were. One afternoon, just after school let out and the

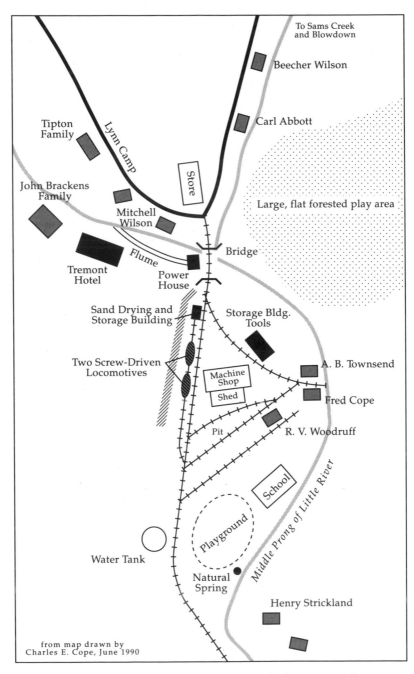

To Sams Creek
and Blowdown

Beecher Wilson

Carl Abbott

Tipton
Family

Lynn Camp

John Brackens
Family

Store

Mitchell
Wilson

Large, flat forested play area

Flume

Bridge

Tremont
Hotel

Power
House

Sand Drying and
Storage Building

Storage Bldg.
Tools

Two Screw-Driven
Locomotives

Machine
Shop

Shed

A. B. Townsend

Fred Cope

R. V. Woodruff

Pit

School

Middle Prong of Little River

Playground

Water Tank

Natural
Spring

Henry Strickland

from map drawn by
Charles E. Cope, June 1990

Map 8. Tremont Settlement. The central camp for loggers and their
families, 1931.

Dorie: Woman of the Mountains

children were walking the railroad home, a roaring wind took trees off the mountains on both sides of them. Anxiously, I watched for them to come into sight. The wind was blowing at their backs and pushing them forward. The roar overhead echoed in the hollows, making it sound as if we were caught in the middle of a great, windy battle. A tornado had struck near Sam's Creek, transforming the timber to rubble and splinters. To this day, that place is called "Blowdown."

Summer brought a phenomenon never seen in the mountains. We awoke one morning to find the camp filled with huge rats. Black rats, brown rats, and spotted rats ran wildly from the river. They were into everything. Baby chicks were killed and partially eaten. Food for the livestock was scattered. Holes gnawed in the feed sacks left grain pouring onto the ground. Before morning was over, they had found every hole and weak spot in our homes. They ran across the floors and under the furniture. Women forgot their squeamishness and were battering them with brooms and mops. Men got guns and clubs to try to herd them away. Every time one was killed, two more showed up to take its place.

All our metal and glass containers were used to protect our food. Lamps stayed lit all night. We didn't dare step out of bed in the darkness. There was no place to keep the livestock food away from the rats. Hundreds were killed. We took sticks, clubs, hoes, or any weapons available when we went outside. I was thankful I didn't have a tiny baby to watch constantly. When we fed the pigs, the rats came in droves to the troughs. They were so greedy, they tumbled into the swill and ate while they swam. The pigs squealed helplessly as food was taken out of their mouths.

The invasion lasted about a month before they went en masse on up the river. We felt a great plague had been called down upon us and was now lifted. Men no longer carried guns every time they went out the door. Sunday afternoons, which had been used as hunting days for the rats, were once again silent and peaceful.

We heard they were Norwegian wharf rats, which had come from a seaport in Louisiana. It was thought that they came up the Mississippi River, the Tennessee River, and eventually into Little River. Almost like one of the plagues in Egypt, they came and went without warning. In spite of the rat invasion, we felt everything was going well on the job.

We hadn't had any serious injuries, but our luck was about to run out. Hobert Proffitt was sitting beside the skidder, eating his lunch with the crew. Above him, the cable holding a newly cut log snapped. The log swung free and crushed him against the skidder. A sad crew brought him home. Ma went to his home to help the family and to prepare him for burial. They dressed him in his overalls and laid him on the bed. Friends and relatives came to comfort his family and to view his body.

Before the shock of Hobert's death wore off, we lost another crew member. Pete McCarter had his neck broken by the handle of a jack. Having lost two men in so short a time was a blow to us. Mountain people believe deaths occur by threes. Who would be the third one, we wondered?

It wasn't long after we'd lost our friends that we began hearing we'd soon lose our jobs, too. Rumors had been circulating through the camp that the Little River Lumber Company was being sold to the government. Wealthy folk in Knoxville had discovered the Smokies, after all those years, and had started a campaign to have the mountains made into a national park. The timber cutting would have to be stopped. We had mixed feelings about the park. We loved the mountains and wanted them to remain beautiful, but the timber was our bread and butter.

Fred knew he wasn't prepared to work at many good-paying jobs. He detested the cotton mills. Whatever he did had to be outdoors. Electric power was a new and promising development. Eventually, it would reach every corner of the country. He answered an advertisement for a correspondence course on electricity, and pamphlets came, painting a glowing picture of the future of electricity. Fred became a student of the Cones Electric School of Chicago.

After a full day's work on the skidder, he'd spend hours study-ing at night. I came to know what "burning the midnight oil" meant. Some of the math problems were more advanced than his ninth-grade education. When he came to a problem he couldn't solve, he took his books and went to see Newt Clabough, my teacher from the Glades and now bookkeeper for the lumber com-pany. Newt worked with him until he understood and worked out the problem.

One of his assignments required him to build a generator for electricity. The school sent him some parts, but we had to make do with some homemade ones, too. He built a trough to carry the water to a wheel, which turned the generator and made electricity. The school had sent two electric light bulbs. Fred ran wires to the middle of the kitchen and sitting room. The naked bulbs hung limp from the ceiling. "Don't touch the bulbs until I get back," Fred said. He went outside and started the generator. "Now, just watch when I snap this switch." Sud-denly the whole room was filled with a clear, steady light many times brighter than the kerosene lamp. It was a miracle. Elec-tricity had come to the Smokies. People came to see our bright lights, which seemed to come from nowhere. How could a little machine and a few wires create such perfect light?

Time slipped by. Fred got a letter from his mother, remind-ing him she hadn't seen him in three or four years. She begged him to come home. We didn't have enough money for train tickets for all of us, so we decided that he should go. The chil-dren and I would stay at home in Stringtown.

When he came back he had a crystal radio set. He had traded his most prized possession, a camera, for it. His brothers-in-law, Horace and Wade Abee, were very enthusiastic about this new invention. Fred wanted us to hear for ourselves. We took turns listening to music from Nashville on the headphones. The mu-sic was faint and laced with the squeaks and squawks of static. It was magic to us because it was a link to the outside world.

Rumor became fact. The Little River Lumber Company lands

were sold to the government. The company still had cutting rights for fifteen years, so we wouldn't be affected soon. However, we made long-range plans to leave the mountains. Nothing changed on the surface, but we knew how the loggers felt about moving out and looking for work. Many of these people had lived their lives in the shadows of the mountain peaks. Generations of ancestors had lived and died here. Now their descendants were displaced citizens with no claim on the land. Eventually, they all would have to go.

Five good years were spent here. We had lived in Stringtown longer than any place since we'd married. Charles would be five years old, and my "second" family was about to begin. On Wednesday, November 9, 1927, William Wayne was born. As usual, Dr. Bruce Montgomery was there with all his bluster, and, as usual, he did nothing to relieve my discomfort. Nature was left to take its course. We hadn't had a baby in the family in so long that Wilma and Edith made a toy out of the curly-haired boy.

When the schoolday was over at Lynn Camp, they'd rush home, each demanding it was "my" day to play with the baby. Lynn Camp School was one of the best we'd had. The children eagerly grabbed a lunch pail filled with biscuits, meat, and jelly or apple butter, and walked to school. Paul still had to be watched to be sure he didn't memorize his reader instead of learning to read word-for-word. His ability to memorize anything he heard was astounding.

Stringtown was a fisherman's paradise. Men had contests to see who could catch the biggest fish. No fish was wasted. When we could, we had them for three meals a day. Orville Ownby won the prize without a doubt. He caught a trout so big it practically filled a wash tub. He was camp celebrity for some time. Ma could still catch more fish than most men, but she never came near Orville's record-size trout.

The children loved Stringtown more than any place we'd lived. When they were grown men, Paul and Charles went back and found the rock where they had played. Holes, tediously drilled by two small boys, were still in the rock.

Christmases came and went. We still didn't have Christmas trees at home, but the company always had a big one for the school party. I bought dolls for the girls and trains for the boys. Ma always gave us enough material for two dresses for each girl and overalls for the boys. Santa Claus was not part of our celebration. The children knew the gifts were bought with hard-earned money and that they just didn't appear miraculously in a stocking or under a tree.

When we left Stringtown, Fred sold the electrical equipment to Creed Spurgeon, who later moved it to Cosby, built his own mill wheel, and became the first man to have electricity there. Once again, we were using kerosene lamps with their soft, flickering glow.

In early January, 1928, we moved, house and all, higher into the mountains to Mark's Cove just below Clingman's Dome. This was the highest peak belonging to Little River Lumber Company. It was the most beautiful place we lived. Just across the Tennessee–North Carolina line above us, the Norwood Lumber Company had burned completely in 1925, and the site had been abandoned. We were the only people for many miles around. Our house was the last one at the end of the line toward Clingman's Dome.

The company built an extra room on the back of our house so we could keep boarders. As always, there were more workers than housing. Four men moved in. I only cooked for them. They took care of their own bedding and clothing. I never knew what they did with their spare time. Every chance they got, they went back down to Tremont where there were more interesting things to do.

A cold, crystal spring ran from the mountain in front of our house. An iron pipe was implanted in the spring, and water ran constantly into a big, galvanized tub. The sun came up in front of the house. While the sky was still dark, silvery streaks appeared over the mountaintops. Later, the sun rose slowly, majestically through trees covered with hoar frost and ice. Each icy tree caught the sunlight and gave back rainbow colors.

Fred worked when the weather permitted. It was so cold that

the loggers had to keep a fire burning in the machine boilers all the time. The temperature was twenty-eight below zero on several occasions. During a hard freeze, the water line to one of the skidders froze and burst. The noise echoed through the mountains like exploding dynamite. When I went to milk in the morning, ice formed on the collar of my coat where I breathed. We had to take special care of the cattle. They could survive the cold during the day but had to have warm stalls at night. One neighbor lost his milch cow. She had gotten out during the night and froze to death. The loss of a cow was devastating. The milk and butter were essential to family health, and usually there was no money to replace her.

A pot-bellied stove kept the one-room school warm on average days, but when the cold wind howled outside, the heat could only be felt if you were very close. Lessons were forgotten as the children huddled around it to keep warm.

There were about twenty children in school. They still drank from one dipper and out of one water bucket. When colds and epidemics came, I took my children out of school. The cemetery at Mark's Creek is full of small graves—children who died of pneumonia, croup, and diseases brought in from the outside. Red measles could kill and did. Unless someone brought in an infectious disease, we stayed well.

On a cold Saturday morning, Fred said he was going to Elkmont to get shoes for all the children. He got a birch stick and measured each small foot, cutting a notch in the stick where each foot reached. He put on his Mackinaw coat, a cap with furry ear flaps, and his work boots. The trip would have to be made on foot. He would be traveling logging trails and trying to go straight "as the crow flies" to get to Elkmont and back before midnight.

All day the children looked for him to return. I kept telling them it was much too soon to expect him back. Darkness came early, with the short winter days. Wind howled through the trees and rattled the windows. I was anxious to have him home, but I kept reassuring the children. It was almost nine o'clock when the wind blew him and the snow through the front door. We all rushed toward him. "Whoa," he said, "I feel like sugar covered with ants." A big, brown package was strapped to his back. He had taken his belt and a piece of string and tied the bundle on his back. He needed his hands free to climb the snow-covered trails, using two short poles for balance.

Wilma and Edith must have been dreaming of shoes like Cinderella's—or, at least, shiny patent-leather slippers. What they got were high-topped, brown shoes and long, olive-green stockings to keep them warm. Disappointment showed in their faces, but they knew he'd done what he thought best. They would be warm and practical for the cold walk to school. Dreams don't always come true. What we want and what we need are two different things—a hard lesson to learn when you're young.

As often happens after a severe winter, spring came early. Fred screened in the porch, and we spent most of our time on it. Edith loved to get up early and watch the sun slip up and over the mountains. The robins were coming back, and wildflowers covered the forest floor.

"Mom, I just saw the most beautiful thing in the world," she said one morning.

"What was it?"

"There was a robin singing in the very top of a tree. The sun behind him made him look like he was framed with gold!"

As the old saying goes: We counted our chickens before they were hatched. Spring seemed so certain and well established that we were completely surprised when snow started falling in May. It started as dainty flurries in the afternoon. By dusk, it had taken on the appearance of a full-grown blizzard. When the wind stopped and morning came, we had several feet of snow. It was no work and all play the rest of the day. We made snow cream by filling glasses with snow, adding sugar, vanilla, and milk, and stirring.

During the warm months, we would go to visit Pa and Ma in Stringtown. Luther and Fred hunted while I heard all the news from Ma and Lola. Ma had many relatives on the job and kept up with all of them. If we wanted to know anything about them, all we had to do was ask her. She always knew who was getting married, who was having babies, and where they were working in the mountains.

Sometime in July, Fred's brothers, Harry and Bob, came looking for work. We put two more bunks in with our boarders. I later learned their real purpose for coming. Bob, especially, couldn't abide "hillbillies," so I should have been suspicious from the start. Their father had sent them to persuade Fred to come back to North Carolina and get rich raising chickens. Everything was settled except for one small detail. Fred hadn't the courage to tell me about the business venture. He was going to have everything ready and simply tell me we were moving. How wrong he was! I wasn't going back to North Carolina.

Many letters went back and forth between Mr. Cope and his sons. Fred never told me what was going on, but I noticed that the letters were always torn to shreds after the three of them had read them. Curiosity rose like yeast inside me. I had to know what was going on. One day, they were working high on the mountain and would be late getting home. As fate would have it, a letter arrived from North Carolina. I couldn't stay away from it. Countless times I picked it up and quickly put it back down. When the supper was cooking on the stove and great, white clouds of steam rose from the pots, a wicked idea completely overcame my better judgment. I picked up the letter and held it in the steam. Slowly, the flap loosened and curled back. I slipped out the letter and read about the master plan.

Once I knew the plan, my strategy was simple. Fred really couldn't keep a secret, and since I knew what to fish for, he didn't have a chance. I sealed the letter back up and set the flat iron over it to press out the telltale creases. When they came in that night, they took the letter and went outside to read it. I watched Bob tear it to shreds and go toward the outhouse to get rid of it.

As I expected, Fred told me everything when I confronted him.

They were amazed I had discovered their plan. It never occurred to them that I had read the letter. It was in perfect shape when they opened it, and it was never out of their hands after it was opened. Very calmly and firmly, I told Fred if he went to North Carolina to raise chickens, he'd go without me. He must have believed me, because he gave up without a struggle. Harry and Bob suddenly decided they could find work on the other side of the mountain.

We were all unhappy when the orders came to leave Mark's Cove. God's handiwork had reached perfection here. The crystal spring water ran icy cold in the hot summer, the trees reached high toward heaven, the rhododendron and mountain laurel grew thick and beautiful under the rocky overhangs, ferns, moss, and an assortment of wildflowers carpeted the ground we walked on. Birds sang lullabies, and squirrels barked out warnings to invaders infringing on their territory. Sometimes at night, we'd hear the spine-chilling scream of a panther or wildcat. Now, in my later years, this is the place that appears most often in my dreams. I can feel the good, cold water in my mouth and the pure, crisp air in my lungs.

The lumber company was being very selective in cutting trees now. Certain standards had to be met before one was cut. A new policy had been put into effect when the land was sold to the government. Instead of scalping the mountain, only the biggest and best trees were taken. As a result, our jobs were for shorter periods of time. We spent less time away from the central locations of Tremont and Elkmont.

With more free time, the men had more time to think up devilish pranks to play on each other. A tale began to circulate about a haunted cabin on one of the hollows near Tremont. The tales became more frightening as they went along. After a few Saturday-night swallows of white lightning, men became brave knights ready to take on any foe, seen or unseen. To make the undertaking more interesting, they collected fifty dollars to give to the man who would stay one whole night in the haunted cabin. The timekeeper, "Punch-out" Gilland, was the volunteer.

He went inside, and the men stretched out on the ground around the cabin to be sure he stayed all night. Everything was quiet until about one in the morning. Punch-out burst out the front door, running at top speed toward the camp with all the men in pursuit. He disappeared into his own house for the rest of the night. In the morning he wouldn't talk about what had happened or what he'd seen. There were no more takers for the fifty-dollar jackpot.

In early spring of 1929, we moved to Sam's Creek, about a mile above Tremont. The children were going to school in Tremont, where Eulah Fox Broome taught. Her husband, Shirley Broome, was a train engineer for the company. With her help, the school had begun to build a small library. This had been a problem in all the schools.

To be sure my children, as well as Fred and I, had books—I ordered one or two every time an order was sent to Sears and Roebuck. We had almost all of Zane Grey's novels and Edgar Rice Burrough's "Tarzan" books. Zane Grey's *Betty Zane* had been read so many times that the covers were pasted and patched together. Gene Stratton-Porter held us captive with her tales of the "Limberlost," a dismal swamp in Indiana. We had *Freckles, A Girl of the Limberlost, The Harvester, Laddie, Her Father's Daughter, Keeper of the Bees,* and *The Song of the Cardinal.* Grace Livingston Hill was a favorite author among the women in camp. She wrote romantic novels. We borrowed and exchanged books with all our friends and relatives. I had read to all the children long before they were old enough to understand what I was reading to them. Fred usually bought a Sunday newspaper. The children and I took turns reading the funny paper aloud.

For the first time in many years, we didn't have boarders to feed. The children and I were free to walk in the woods, play in the streams, or just daydream. Life for me was drastically different from the way Ma's had been. We bought what we wanted from the company store or ordered from Sears and Montgomery Ward. We still canned and preserved our food, but I never had to weave anything to wear. My children never gave me much trouble. I felt as young and free-spirited as they acted. In truth, I had started my family when I was so young, I felt I had grown up with them.

On the weekend, we sometimes went to the movies in Tremont. The children begged to go, since this was a new, fascinating form of entertainment for them. Charles, seven at the time, never seemed to understand they weren't real. In one movie, a train broke loose and ran wildly down the track—seemingly coming toward us. Closer and closer it appeared on the screen. Charles watched in horror, screamed, and hid under the seat. His movie watching was over for awhile.

The school board got every film they could beg or borrow. One came from the county agricultural department. This film would give you an idea how much we wanted entertainment and enlightenment. It was a whole story showing the destructiveness of the corn borer. The villain was a farmer named Jones who wouldn't listen to the pleading of the agriculture department to burn his corn stalks, infected by the borer. All his neighbors did as they were told—but not Farmer Jones. He let his corn grow and harvested what he could. Ah, but he had trouble! One morning, he got up and found holes everywhere. His wife stepped off the back porch and disappeared down a hole. His barn had holes. His house had holes. It seemed the corn borer was no longer interested in corn but in everything on his farm. The last scenes showed Farmer Jones awakening from his nightmare and dutifully burning his corn and the horrible borer.

Since there was no real pasture land and not much to eat, our cattle roamed free in the camp. There were no fences anywhere. Trains would stop for cattle on the tracks. Newt Ownby had a big, black bull that thought the whole territory belonged to him. He'd come to our house and run the children inside. After they came into the house, he'd paw around and butt at the timber supporting our back porch, causing the house to shake. I felt sure he'd send us and the house tumbling down the mountain if the posts came loose. We had no defense against him. The children played with caution outside—always aware that he'd be upon them before they could get out of his way.

On his next visit, I had a surprise waiting for him. I saw him charge into the yard, snorting and pawing. All the children seemed to come through the door at the same time. As usual, our porch post was his next target. He was so angry and aggressive that his onslaught caused the dishes to rattle on the shelves. I took the kettle of boiling water off the stove, slipped quietly out onto the back porch, leaned over the railing, and poured the steaming water all over him. He bellowed and went charging up the mountain. He never came back to bother us. Sometimes he'd stand across the tracks and look at our house. I often wondered what he was thinking.

Heavy thunderstorms had started early in the spring. Strong winds battered the mountainsides but never reached tornado strength here. After one hard storm, the children went out to play. Minutes later, they were back inside begging me to come and see what was outside. They had found tiny frogs all over the ground. The frogs were so small they looked like spiders hopping around. We decided it must have rained frogs. Probably a wind funnel had sucked them up from a pond or river and had released them in the storm over the mountains. Ma had told us an old English legend about a tree that grew fish. They found that the wind had blown them to the tree, and it didn't grow them at all. That, surely, was the reason it "rained" frogs. For a long time, the children looked for frogs every time it rained. We never saw them again.

I don't know if the warm, heavy rains were the cause, but the loggers were having more trouble than usual with snakes this summer. Copperheads and rattlers were everywhere. One day, the saw ripped through a partially dead tree, and, when it fell, the men counted twenty-two copperheads cut in half.

During a heavy rain on a cool morning, Fred took cover under a hanging rock. Noticing what he thought was a pile of sticks and leaves, he reached down for a stick and drew back his hand in horror. He was standing beside a pile of copperheads. The cold weather had made them sluggish, or he would have been bitten. Twenty-six snakes were taken from the pile. A few days later, he reached under a log to fasten a chain around it. When the log was lifted high, a four-foot copperhead dangled from the bottom. He'd put the chain around the snake, too. Pa kept a record of the snakes in his time book. Before the summer was over, the crew had killed 354 snakes—copperheads and rattlers.

Bears were a problem, too. Several cows had been killed and pigs carried off. One family found their cow with part of its hindquarters eaten away, but, somehow, it was still alive. Of course, it had to be killed. A full-grown bear standing upright could carry a pig in its front paws, cradled like a baby in its mother's arms.

The men in camp planned to hunt and kill as many bears as they could find. Paul went to Pa's to borrow a rifle for the hunt and was gone longer than we thought he should be. Fred started up the railroad to see if there was any trouble. Just as he was passing a high bank on his left, something jumped off the bank and landed at his feet, missing him by inches. He held the light high in front of him. Just steps away, a black panther lay panting. He stepped back to get some distance from it, then he ran like the wind. Apparently, the panther had jumped at him and missed. It struck the railroad tracks, addling itself. Looking back, he saw the black form stumbling toward the river. The next morning, we all went to look for tracks. Panther tracks as big as my hand went down the bank to the water.

Nature seemed determined to cause trouble on this job. Several small earthquakes rumbled under our feet—just enough to make us nervous and watchful. In late July, a heavier quake shook the mountains. Our back bedroom broke loose from the rest of the house. We were outside in seconds. Panic kept us up all night. The children sat big-eyed and silent in the dimly lit room. We were not in the mood for games or small talk.

Soon after the children started to school in September, Fred was caught in the worst accident of his logging career. I saw four men coming toward the house carrying a limp body. When someone was hurt on the job, he was taken to the nearest house for care and to wait for Dr. Montgomery if the injury was bad.

It wasn't until they were almost in the house that I knew it was Fred. His pant legs were torn, and blood oozed from blue, puffy blotches below his knees. The skin was scraped from his cheek and down one arm. We were not sure which bones were broken or how many.

Impatience had been his undoing. The crew had been working the same section for several hours. The skidder had hauled many logs from the side of the mountain, and the pile was high. They decided to go for one more load. The skidder operator pulled the burden of logs upon the side of the pile and had backed off on the cable so the chokers could be unlocked. Looking around for the choker "expert" and not seeing him, Fred decided to do it himself. He climbed up the pile and had unhooked about half of the chokers when the logs began to slide. Fred lost his balance and fell into the log pile. He lay sprawled across a large log. The choker cable with a log still attached was across both his legs. He lay hanging head down from the top of the pile, while the cable crushed his legs with the weight of a huge log pulling on the other end.

Allen Sizemore quickly saw the problem. He picked up a double-bit ax and in one stroke cut the cable. Free from the burden of the log, the cable whipped and curled upward, un-pinning Fred who tumbled down the side of the pile.

It was a miracle that his legs were not broken, but much damage was done to the muscles. Before it was over, the massive bruises turned almost every color of the rainbow. It was many weeks before he could work again. He didn't get any pay while he was off, and again our meager savings were used up. While he was getting well, he studied books about electricity. Besides working for the lumber company, Allen Sizemore was a Baptist Preacher. He and his co-workers kept us fed while Fred's leg mended. They brought in boxes of food until Fred's salary was started again.

Signs of fall were all around us now, and, with the changing of the seasons, election time was coming. Fred had always encouraged me to vote. He took me to Tremont to register and pay the poll tax. It was a presidential election year and Fred wanted us to hear all the speeches. He ordered a battery radio from Sears. Everybody went to Tremont to vote and came back to our house that night to hear the results. We had the only radio on the job. The house and yard were full of people, Democrats and Republicans, each sure if their candidate didn't win, the world was doomed.

Warren G. Harding was the first man I voted for, Calvin Coolidge the next. This time I voted for Herbert Hoover. Every man I had voted for won the presidency, a pretty good average for a beginner, I thought. However, I was not so lucky with my votes for many years after that.

Fred finished his studies with Cones Electric School and took his new knowledge to Knoxville in search of a job. The lumber business was being phased out, and the men were leaving the mountains. The Tennessee Public Service Company hired him. They were building a power line from Knoxville to Waterville, North Carolina. He would have to stay on the job all week and come home on the weekends. Wilma and Paul were ready for high school, so we were going to have to move where schooling was available. Pittman Center was the nearest place.

Fred went to Pittman to find a house. He rented a small, white house and hired a man with a truck to come back with him and move us. The house was much better than the one we were living in on the job. The sitting room had a fireplace. When we were settled and everything was in place, Fred went to Waterville to begin his new work.

Pittman Center is back-to-back with the Great Smoky Mountains National Park. Many mountaineers had sold their land to the government and moved to Pittman. The increased population showed up in the schools. For the first time, my children went to different schools, instead of all being together in one room. Edith and Charles went to Pittman Grammar School, while Paul and Wilma attended the high school. Hot lunches were served at the school, and it had a good library.

Pittman School had been the project of the Methodist Board of Home Missions. Dr. Robert Thomas had come into the area as a medical missionary years before. The school and clinic had been built with Methodist money and mountaineer muscle. He and his wife cared for the the sick in the clinic and made housecalls into the deep hollows and coves.

After Fred went to Waterville, the children and I took care of each other. We had never been without Fred except the time I had left him alone in Eldorado and the week he visited his family in North Carolina. The library supplied us with enough books to read. On cool days, we kept a fire in the fireplace. I baked bread in a Dutch oven on the hearth and cooked beans in a kettle over the fire—the way Ma cooked in Oconaluftee before she got a stove. We had a stove, but it was fun sitting around the fire, waiting for supper.

In the larger schools, the children were exposed to more sickness. Colds and sore throats plagued us all fall. Edith became very sick with a cough and a fever. I told Paul to go by Dr. Thomas's office and ask him to come by to see her. In the after noon, I answered a knock at the door and saw a tall, gentle-looking man smiling at me. He examined Edith and turned to me. He wanted to examine me because I was very pregnant and very tired. I wasn't used to having medical attention before I gave birth.

He told me I had an enlarged heart and should be very careful. In fact, I shouldn't even be out of bed. I was scared to death. What would become of my children if something happened to me? I had always asked God to let me live until they didn't need

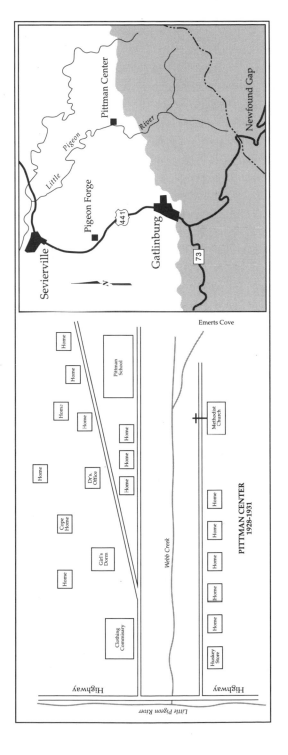

Map 9. Pittman Center is built in a flood plain. Flash floods can come without warning, sometimes with tragic results. Once houses dotted the hillsides, with footpaths leading from the roads running on both sides of the creek.

me anymore. It was unthinkable that they might have a step-mother. At first, I stayed in bed all I could with five children to care for. As time passed and I felt everything was going to be all right, I didn't stay in bed anymore.

Dr. Thomas made regular visits to see me. We lived on a hill and could see him when he started up the trail. Before he got to the door, I'd get into bed and try to look comfortable and rested when he came in. He thought I was a good patient and following his orders.

The months passed, and Fred's job in Waterville was almost over. He said the company wanted him to go to Memphis to finish work there. He came home to get us ready to move, but I didn't want to go. I was in the last stages of pregnancy, and Dr. Thomas's warning about my heart hung like a dark cloud over my head. After much discussion, we decided he would go alone. So he left, not knowing when he would come back home. There was no choice—he had to go where he could earn a living.

It was a blessing that we didn't go with him. The job lasted a little over three months. We hadn't been able to save any money. He had to pay room and board there, and I had to maintain a home for five children here. When he got back to Knoxville, he learned that there was no more work for anyone. He was laid off. The depression was tightening its grip on the country. Things were to get much worse before they got better.

Fred's brother, Harry, came looking for work. Together they went begging for anything to do. Harry was a good-natured man who talked a blue streak. He liked to stay at our house because he said it was the only place he could get three hot meals a day.

Harry (the children called him Uncle Fuzz) was shocked when he saw Wayne in light brown curls, hanging to his shoulders. He was sure we had ruined him for life—doomed him to sissyhood. Three years old and he still looked like a girl! Wilma and Edith wouldn't let anyone touch his head of bouncy curls. But Harry won out. He took Wayne for a walk, and, when he came back, there wasn't a curl to be seen. His beautiful hair was cropped and uneven all over his head. The girls were furious. Of course, they couldn't be disrespectful to their uncle, but if looks could kill, he'd be dead!

Wayne just smiled and didn't seem to care either way. He was a bright child who sang all the time. His sisters' attention had helped him talk before he was a year old. He knew all the words to the hymns we sang. His small, clear voice drifted from wherever he happened to be playing alone. But he never seemed alone. His ears rang with music only he could hear.

He loved peach pie and "rossen ears" (baked corn on the cob) more than anything. He seemingly disappeared one afternoon, and we hunted and called for him for what seemed like hours. Paul said, "If he's in hearing distance, I know what to do!" He started calling, "Wayne, do you want a rossen ear?" A sleepy scamp came crawling out from under a bed, where we thought we'd already searched. He was fighting mad when he didn't get his corn!

When we had peach pie, he usually got more than his share. Aunt Sally Bright was coming for supper, and I made a cobbler pie. Wayne sat looking at Aunt Sally and then at the pie. After mentally measuring the servings, he knew he wouldn't get his usual generous amount. He looked up at Aunt Sally and said in a firm voice, "You don't like peach pie, do you." It wasn't a question. It was a warning! Aunt Sally had a good sense of humor. She laughed and wasn't offended.

On April 24, 1930, I awoke with a very familiar feeling. The baby was coming. Fred went to Dr. Thomas's office and asked him to come and help me. The doctor had asked to be called as soon as my labor started. He wanted to watch my progress and save my heart from too much stress. When it was time, he put a mask over my face and poured drops of ether into the gauze. The strong, burning odor seemed to reach every nerve in my body. My head felt light and wobbly. I drifted off to sleep. My son, Dwight Arnold, was born as I floated on downy clouds. This beautiful child came without the discomfort that has been woman's lot since Eve.

I never had been treated with such kindness and concern. Mrs. Eva Thomas, the doctor's wife, came every day to bathe me and the baby. She brought food and changed my bed linen. She taught me to cook several new dishes. The one I remember most is Spanish rice. Dr. Thomas brought material to make a crib. Students in the high school workshop class had cut it out, ready to be put together. Paul made it and painted it white. I folded one of my heaviest quilts to use as a mattress. My first and only baby crib stood beside my bed, white and lovely, while my tiny, red-faced son slept like a kitten in the middle.

No work was available anywhere, and our money had disappeared long ago. The food on our pantry shelves was going fast in spite of our attempts to make it last as long as possible. Fred hunted small game to keep meat on the table. Our twenty-gallon crock of pickled corn was gone. A few bundles of leather britches (dried green beans) hung from the ceiling.

All the flat land, or what we called "bottom land," from Pittman Center to Newport was used to grow beans and tomatoes for the big Stokely Brothers cannery in Newport. They canned their produce in tin cans—cans we couldn't afford to buy.

One fall afternoon during Paul's youthful, restless wanderings, he found tomatoes in the tall grass around the cannery fields. They were under the thick covering of grass that had fallen and protected them from the killing frosts which left the ones in the fields inedible. He stuffed his shirt full and came home with his bounty. We had fried green tomatoes, stewed tomatoes, tomatoes with biscuits, and tomatoes we ate whole like apples. They were the best-tasting tomatoes I ever had in my whole life!

We were at our lowest ebb. Never had we been so close to starvation. Of course, we were not alone. The whole world seemed to stand still. No work, no money, and very little hope.

Wilma worked for Dr. and Mrs. Thomas a few days a week. She helped do the laundry and household chores. Her pay was small, but it was better than nothing.

We were all tired. The girls never complained about their old clothes. We all ate less. The saddest of all was that we almost forgot how to laugh. Our house always rang with laughter over minor, silly things. When one funnybone was tickled, we all dissolved into uncontrollable hilarity. Now, I couldn't remember when laughter had last filled the house.

Worry and work left me ill. Dr. Thomas came, knowing he would not be paid for his work. After examining me, he took Fred outside and told him I was very sick. I was anemic, and my heart was enlarged and overworked. He said I'd probably be dead in three months. Those three remaining months would have to be spent in bed. Not knowing what to do, Fred wrote Ma in Tremont and, for the first time, asked for advice.

She told him to bring me home. We could move in with them until a house was ready for us. It was doubtful that the lumber company would hire Fred since their business was at a standstill, too. Ma said the new company doctor, Edward W. Griffin, was well liked and she had much faith in him.

Dr. Montgomery had already moved to Gatlinburg and opened an office there. I had not seen the last of this man who had been so much a part of our lives.

So many of my years had been spent in and near Tremont, I really felt I was coming home. But not to die, Dear Lord! I couldn't go and leave my babies. I prayed without ceasing, pleading for my life. Dr. Griffin came to see me after Fred went to his office and told him I was sick. I was very anemic, and, indeed, my heart was enlarged, but could it be heredity? The first thing he wanted me to do was eat properly and have a drink of brandy twice a day to build up my strength. We sent to Maryville for a bottle of brandy. It was expensive and, I felt, a waste.

Fred became a "moonshiner" temporarily. He found a recipe for peach brandy and made a batch. We had plenty of free advice and offers to taste our brew. I never drank the brandy. My puritanical background convinced me that it was sinful and that surely God could heal me without the peach spirits.

Slowly my health improved. Being in my beloved mountains, among friends and relatives, gave me courage. Everything was familiar here. We were soon settled into a routine, almost as if we'd never been away from the logging camps. Many of the people were gone, and only a few isolated cuttings were being done. Most of the work was on the tracks and in the railroad shop. Ernest and Bernice Headrick still ran the hotel.

Fred went into the company office to ask about work. They weren't hiring anybody. The operation was being slowly closed down. As he left the office, he met D. H. (Doc) Tipton. Mr. Tipton had always been a good friend. He asked Fred what he was doing back in Tremont. "Looking for a job," Fred said, "but they won't hire me." "Go back in there and tell them I said to put you to work," Mr. Tipton told him. Fred got the job. He went to work with Pa, maintaining the railroad.

Pa's time books list a crew of twenty-five for October 1931 when Fred started to work. The November crew was cut to six men. From then until 1935, only six to ten people were listed. Fred stayed on the payroll for four months. In March 1932, the Tennessee Electric Power Company called him back to help build power lines between Sevierville and Gatlinburg.

All my family lived in a row—Am and Lola, Luther and Willie, Pa and Ma with us. Our house was the last one near the river across from Buckeye Flats. The school was behind us, about halfway between the river and the railroad.

Am Townsend teased my children unmercifully. They loved every minute of it. Even in the coldest weather he'd say to one of them, "If you'll come over to my house, we'll cut a watermelon." The older ones knew he was teasing, but the younger ones followed him home only to be told, "Oh, we're too late. Somebody else ate it."

On one of his trips to Elkmont, he brought back two rabbits. He gave Paul a black one and Charles a gray one. The gray one got out and never came back. The black one stayed and ruled the whole house. We never gave him a name, he was just "Rabbit." He came and went as he pleased. The cats scattered when he came in the door. There wasn't one of them that didn't have scars from his strong hind feet. Rabbit had his own place at the table and his own tin plate. He'd stand or sit on his hind feet in a chair and eat out of the plate on the table. The smell of supper brought him in from distant hideouts. Huckleberry pie drove him into a frenzy. Afterwards, he'd lick his paws until all the evidence of his greediness was gone. Everybody knew and loved him and, I suppose, coveted him as a pet. People were moving out of the mountains, and we think someone took Rabbit with them when they left camp. We never found him. When we heard anything that sounded like the familiar scratches at the door, we ran to open it, only to be disappointed.

The rabbit was only one of many pets in the family. Ma had a small dog, Fannie, which killed every snake she could find. We saw her many times in a life-and-death battle with a thrashing, hissing serpent. She had the uncanny ability to know how far a snake could strike. She'd stay far enough away to escape the fangs and grab it before it could coil and strike again.

We also had a frustrated sheepdog. He was excellent at rounding up the cows and bringing them home. There was one problem—he'd get the time mixed up and bring them home in the middle of the day. We herded them back to the open pasture and wondered how we could teach a dog to tell time.

We had to keep a careful eye on our cattle. Bears were a problem, but the railroad cars caused more damage. When the work trains caused damage, we accepted that as part of the job hazards. The company's fancy Chrysler Runabout Convertible, which had been mounted on the railroad tracks, was a different story. It was used to transport important guests to and from the Tremont Hotel. Out-of-state company officials and their ladies were frequent visitors, along with the wealthy investors from Knoxville. Our feelings toward the hotel were not helped any when the car hit our only young heifer, Snowball. The loss of a milch cow is a great loss to a family that cannot afford to replace her.

This Chrysler Runabout, mounted on the railroad tracks, was used to bring pampered guests to the Tremont Hotel in the Smoky Mountains in the early 1930s. This car hit the Cope's calf and broke her leg.

Snowball's mother, Old Nell, had died giving birth to her. Fred had even persuaded Dr. Montgomery to come and see if he could do anything to save Old Nell or the baby. Dr. Montgomery's medical knowledge didn't cover bovine anatomy, and the mother died. Snowball was very white and pink. Ma said she was an albino. We mixed cornmeal with milk donated by the neighbors and took turns feeding the little calf twenty-four hours a day. When she was old enough to eat on her own, we thought we had reached a milestone. But we discovered that Snowball had other problems, too. She was stone deaf.

Months of worry had gone into raising Snowball to where she was almost ready to have her first calf and provide us with much-needed milk for the children. Neighbors had been sharing their milk and butter with us. We were grateful for their generosity, but, with Snowball, we had hopes of coming off the dole.

On one of its weekend excursions, about a mile below the

The Tremont Hotel did not receive many guests during the winter months. Lumber company officials had quarters there.

hotel, the Chrysler hit Snowball. She couldn't hear the car horn and didn't move off the tracks. The car wouldn't stop for her. Her leg was broken.

Everybody told Ma the little calf would have to be killed, but Ma wouldn't hear of it. She looked around for two strong trees. As luck would have it, the ones she needed were just feet away from the railroad track. The calf would hardly have to be moved at all. Ma went to the railroad repair shop and got several wide leather strips and two chains. She made a harness for the calf and, with the help of four men lifting the frightened beast, fastened the harness on the calf and the chains around the trees.

This train was reserved for special guests who came to the Wonderland Resort Hotel at Elkmont. Their visits were usually confined to the weekends.

Snowball was suspended between the trees and swayed back and forth while Ma put splints on the broken leg.

The heifer stayed there six weeks, with Ma and all of us taking turns feeding her. Ma still had a mind of her own, and it did no good to tell her that something couldn't be done. To tell her that was akin to waving a red flag in front of an angry bull.

The company never gave us compensation for the damage done to any of our livestock. Their feeling was the same about Snowball—we should keep her off the track. Our attitude toward the hotel and the Chrysler changed to hostility. We had maintained an aloof indifference to the glowing, white-coated building until now.

Dorie: Woman of the Mountains

The Tremont Hotel was situated across the railroad, imbedded into the side of the mountain. The front porch was placed so the visitors had the best possible view of the river and the mountains. The Tremont settlement, with its boxcar, portable housing, and work sheds was out of visual range of the hotel guests.

Settlement people knew the hotel was off limits to them. But that was all right. Mountaineers wouldn't go anyplace they didn't feel welcome. They understood that the rich were different. That was a part of life they couldn't change. By now, most were aware of the differences between the two classes. Many of them had lived near the Wonderland Hotel in Elkmont where the same system worked. The Wonderland was a place to wonder about and view with some envy, as the ladies from Knoxville and other far away cities sat on the front porch in their finery and daintily fanned the gnats and flies away from their perfumed, painted faces.

The rumors and stories of what went on in the hotels kept the natives entertained. Some thought of them as the Sodom and Gomorrah of the mountains. A few local girls were employed as maids at both hotels. Pretty, young daughters were warned to stay away from the places.

Charles came in one day and announced that he had eaten lunch at the hotel. Always the one ready for a new adventure, I believed he had done exactly that. It turned out that Eulah Broome had taken him over there to eat because he had forgotten to take his lunch to school. Mrs. Broome sometimes went to the hotel to eat her lunch while the children in her school were on their own lunch break.

We didn't hold grudges against those who could go to the hotels. In fact, D. H. Tipton came to our rescue many times when we needed help and didn't know where to get it. He arranged for Edith and me to have medical attention at the Acuff Clinic in Knoxville. Edith had a strange, brown spot on her eye. Dr. Griffin thought it might be cancer, and he wanted her to

have special attention. Mr. Tipton drove Fred and Edith to Knoxville and waited until they were ready to come home. Another
time, he took Fred and me to the clinic when I needed surgery
on my leg. Doc was a good man who was always ready to go the
extra mile with people who needed him.

The winter of 1931 was unusually warm for the mountains.
In Pa's company time book, he notes: "March 9, 1932, the first
cold wave and snow for this winter." The lack of snow made
it easier for Fred to come home on the weekends. He stayed
in a boardinghouse during the week and rode the bus from
Maryville to Tremont every Friday night.

We watched more and more people moving out of the mountains. Pa had bought another farm on Middle Creek Road, about
two miles from Pigeon Forge. He had been able to keep the
upper farm during the depression, although he had lost the
money on deposit in the Sevierville bank. The lumber company
had made it possible for him to become a fairly prosperous
landowner. In the fall of 1932, Luther and Willie moved to the
new farm. Lola and Am bought a house in Pigeon Forge.

In the spring of 1933, everything was in bloom by the middle
of March. I couldn't remember seeing blackberry briars covered
with blooms so early. Paul said maybe God was giving us a sign
that everything would be all right. We needed assurance that
spring. Since I had discovered I was pregnant again, I had wondered what would happen in March when my child was born.

Dr. Thomas had said I should never have another child. He
didn't think my heart would stand the strain. When I felt the
first labor pain, Dr. Griffin came to stay with me. I was slow,
and the hours dragged by. Dr. Griffin checked me and said it
would be awhile yet. He went into the back room and went to
bed with the boys. About three in the morning (March 29), I
called out to him. He was at my bedside immediately. After a
shot in the arm, I remember nothing.

When I woke and collected my thoughts, I asked about the
baby. It was a girl. We hadn't had a girl since Edith was born

thirteen years before. Wilma wanted to name her Vida because her best friend was Vida Reagan. I added "Florence" because I liked the name. So, Vida Florence joined our family. Dwight came and sat on the foot of my bed. He'd look at his new sister and then into my face. Big, silent tears rolled down his cheeks. He didn't say a word. I felt I had betrayed him. None of my other children reacted like that at the sight of a new baby in the family. He just wasn't ready to give up his babyhood.

The big news in camp was about a stranger who had come into the area and was living in the railroad sandhouse. The sandhouse was a small building where sand was heated to dry it. All the trains used sand for traction on the mountain tracks. It helped them go up a hill without spinning. The company had given him permission to live in the house.

Charles was very curious about him. When he wasn't fishing, he was at the railroad sandhouse making a pest of himself. The visitor was Professor Rose from the Cincinnati Museum. The government had given him permission to collect two specimens of any flowers in the park. When school was out, he asked if Charles could go with him to collect flowers. Every morning, Charles met him at the sandhouse. They usually came back at noon so the professor could pack his specimens in wet moss and ship them to Ohio.

It wasn't long until the professor came to our house to meet Charles and eat breakfast. At Charles's urging, I had asked him to eat with us anytime he would. His interest in mountain food was boundless. He combed the area for greens and berries. He brought the wild strawberries to us so we would share our cream with him. Each rare find made him glow with pleasure. He found an orchid-type rhododendron on a cliff behind the store. Gold wouldn't have made a prospector happier! He kept saying it was a mistletoe mutation—whatever that meant.

The loggers and railroaders had lived among the flowers and shrubs all their lives. To them, there was nothing special about flora and fauna. The botanist evoked more than a few raised eyebrows and smiles. He seemed strange—that was all; just a polished, educated man among rough, laboring lumbermen.

He and Charles hiked up Blanket Mountain on one last trip before he left. They were gone all day. As the sun set and the mountain shadows lengthened, I became concerned. Professor Rose was an inexperienced outsider, and Charles was a babe in the woods. Almost anything could have happened. My main fear was snakebite.

At dusk, they came wearily down the railroad, both with flowers and plants in every pocket and hand. I knew they must be starved. They hadn't taken anything to eat. Charles said they were too high on the mountain to come in for lunch. Professor Rose had found a rusty gallon can, open on one end, and used it as a soup kettle. They gathered herbs, greenery, and ramps to cook. After washing them in an icy spring, they put them all together in the boiling water, vowing it would be the best soup ever. After a few bites, they decided they really weren't very hungry after all!

As a parting gift, Professor Rose took Charles to the store and bought him an ice cream cone. He didn't have much trouble choosing. The store only had three flavors—vanilla, chocolate, and strawberry. We all missed the professor, but Charles seemed lost without him. All the hiking and attention from the professor had made an interesting summer and left a void that would be hard to fill.

Friendships came easily to the people in Tremont. All the children had best friends. We were all equally poor in money but rich in spirit, so there was very little envy or jealousy. Edith adored Nadine Townsend and spent every spare minute with her. She had begged to spend the weekend with Nadine, but I made excuses to keep her home. I never liked my children to be away from home. Finally, I gave in. She and Nadine spent the whole weekend playing outside without a sweater. When she came home Sunday evening, she was coughing and feverish. In the morning, it was evident she had pneumonia. Dr. Griffin came and left quinine tablets to keep the fever down. There was nothing he could do about the congestion and the disease ravaging her lungs. He stopped by that night and took her temperature again. He didn't say how high it was, but the look of defeat on his face told me she was very sick.

As soon as he left, I got out the skillet and melted about a half-cup of lard. I used all the onions in my house and Ma's during the night. As one hot poultice cooled, I replaced it with a steaming one from the stove. When she awoke in the morning, she felt better. Dr. Griffin came early and checked her temperature. It was down. He shook his head in disbelief and asked what I had done for her. When I told him about the onion poultice, he laughed and said they didn't teach that in medical school, but maybe they should.

All the children were in school except Dwight and Flo, of course. Dwight was a happy youngster, always busy in mind and body. Bursting into the house, he'd tell me fantastic stories or announce, "Mom, I'm going across the river and climb a green tree." (His green tree came out sounding like "gene chee.") Or he would proclaim for all the neighbors to hear, "Roy said a bad word. Roy said a bad word! Do you believe it, Mom?" "Yes, I believe it, Son," I would reply, "but don't you say it." We didn't use profane or obscene words in our family, and that was why it was so fascinating to him.

His friend Roy Tipton drowned in the river just below Tremont. Roy's father was Jabe Tipton, who worked with Pa on the railroad. The settlement was in mourning. Next to croup and pneumonia, the river claimed more children's lives than anything else. God had spared me the tragedy that struck so many families.

One Saturday night we were all in bed when someone pounded on the door. Fred got up to see who it was. A man was standing there with a land deed in his hand. He wanted Fred to buy it because he was in need of fast money. Fred had enough to pay what he was asking for the land, but he said, "No, that land will never be worth anything." Sadly, the man left to knock on another door. "What did he try to sell you?" I asked. "Some land on the river road in Gatlinburg," he said.

Bears still roamed the camps. On Sam's Creek, one had trapped a cow in a pile of logs and attacked her. The park service had already issued an order that no wild animals were to be killed or trapped. A few bears had been killed illegally. Mostly, the bear dogs were silenced and the guns put away. We heard there would be regulations for fishing the streams that had been ours for generations.

In 1934 and 1935, many young men came into the Smokies. A program had started in the depression years for hiring young men to work for the Department of the Interior, under which the park service operated. As more land was acquired for the park, more members of the Civilian Conservation Corps (CCC) set up camps in the mountains. These boys built hiking and horseback trails, fire control roads, fire towers and, in general, tried to erase the scars left by man on the face of the mountains. During the first days of rugged living, several big-city boys left the camp, which was run like an army camp.

The boys wore ill-fitting, olive-drab uniforms and were responsible for their own laundry. Wilma and I washed and ironed shirts for the officers, who liked heavy starch and razor-sharp creases in the sleeves and three creases up the back. I kept three heavy, black irons on the hot stove all day. The shirts needed a strong right arm and plenty of heat to make them "officer" neat. They paid me twenty cents for each shirt.

The CCCs brought their own doctor, a wild sort who drove his car over the mountain roads at top speeds. He was known to have driven the car where there were no roads at all—over cliffs and through underbrush. Totally ignoring curves in the road, he always tried for the shortest distance between two points. As boring as some found life in the camps, they wouldn't ride with him to town on Saturday night. They preferred, instead, to ride the railroad trolley provided by the government.

A tall, blond young man started to visit Wilma. He was with the CCCs, but he was also a local boy. His family had lived in Cosby for generations. They had met at church. Wilma was helping with the collection, and, when she passed his pew, he winked at her. She made a face at him and ignored further attention. She saw him again that afternoon at the river where all the young people met for social get-togethers.

The food at the CCC camp must have been awful—he was always hungry and looked longingly at the cornbread and biscuits on the table. He tried to bribe Dwight and Flo into relinquishing their share. His manners were impeccable. Wilma said he left our table hungry because he was ashamed to eat all he wanted. Eli Thomas Williamson was about to become my son-in-law.

They eloped in September 1934. Reverend Russell Love married them in the Methodist parsonage in Pigeon Forge. I wasn't at all surprised when she came home to tell me. After he married, Tommy wasn't eligible for the CCCs anymore, so he worked with Pa a few months before buying a house in Pigeon Forge.

The last entry in Pa's time book was August 1935. Ma and Pa were moving into the house with Luther on the farm. We moved into the house they vacated, because it was bigger and better than ours. The lumber company didn't charge us rent. A lot of people who lived in Tremont worked somewhere else.

School buses came to take the children to Townsend. Cars and buses replaced the belching, lumbering trains as transportation. Fred had bought a T-Model Ford when he worked in Waterville, but it had been too expensive to maintain and nobody else had enough money to buy it. Paul drove it around Tremont until it collapsed from lack of care. Anything under the hood of a car confused Fred. It was a pile of whirring, chugging machinery that defied man's comprehension.

In 1935, a flu-like epidemic swept through the mountains taking the lives of children under four years old. It was so virulent, it killed its victims in two or three days. Three babies in Tremont had already died when Flo had the first symptoms.

High fever and a hacking cough were the external symptoms. Her lungs were badly damaged and would remain so for the rest of her life. When the news came in, thirteen babies in the Elkmont, Tremont, and Walker's Valley sections were dead. Again, God had spared my child but not without suffering.

There were no wonder drugs or miracle cures, only fever-reducing drugs to help you feel better until the disease ran its course. Human beings are never so helpless as when they watch a child struggling to hold onto life. There's only God and you and the child. If God doesn't extend His mercy, you lose.

I awoke at one in the morning, August 28, with a very familiar feeling. My eighth child was on the way. As soon as daylight came, I got up and started work. I scrubbed the living room and kitchen floors and baked cookies for the children. About eight, I sent Edith to call the doctor and to ask Eldina Wilson to come down to stay with me. She was a midwife. I knew I had waited too long before calling the doctor. My son, Don LeVerne, was born about nine o'clock—twenty minutes before Dr. Griffin came. Don was the only baby born with coal-black hair. I named him LeVerne after Dr. Thomas's son.

Our last winter in the mountains set in with a fury—making up for all the mild ones we'd had. Snow came thick and heavy, with winds blowing it through the cracks in the house. We'd wake up and shake snow off the bed covers. The floors would have a light, powdery snow cover. When I got up to make a fire, I'd leave footprints trailing behind.

For days at a time, the school buses couldn't get through. Fred spent most of his weekends at the boardinghouse, with no way to get home.

After one blizzardy night, I started breakfast in the kitchen and came back to bed bundled in quilts to keep warm. Fred had bought goldfish for me, and I had set them on the shelf for safekeeping from the cats and the children. I loved to watch their golden bodies glide effortlessly through the water. It had a peaceful, tranquilizing effect on me. This morning, they seemed too still. I wondered how they could remain in one place so long. The water looked cloudy, and, when I picked up the bowl, I discovered it was frozen solid. Hopefully, I could thaw them out before they died, if they hadn't already. After pouring warm water over the ice, it cracked and thawed. The fish swam as if nothing had happened.

VI

1937–1942

In March 1937, we left Tremont for the last time. Pa wrote that we could move to the upper farm on Middle Creek. It would be nearer Fred's job, and the boys could do some farming. The activities around Tremont were almost over. Soon, it would be dismantled and moved out as the park claimed the land.

So, for the fourth time, we traveled the narrow, crooked road into the hollow on Middle Creek. The house looked the same as it had the first time. The giant oak stood tall and serene by the roadside. I looked at it with envy–it never bowed in defeat no matter how rough the times. Drought, storms, ice and snow didn't seem to touch it. Why, I wondered. Then the answer came—roots.

Roots was the answer. It had stood in the same place and grown strong, sending roots deep into the earth, while we had moved all over the mountains, even back into North Carolina. In the ten years we'd been gone from this place, we had lived at Jake's Creek, Wildcat Flats, Stringtown, Mark's Cove, Sam's Creek, Pittman Center, and Tremont. Our roots were like those of a fragile flower that only lives one season before it is pulled up and cast aside.

Fred and the boys planted the fields and tobacco acreage. Fred worked with the power company during the week, while the boys cleared the new ground, plowed, harrowed, and planted. There was very little talk at the supper table. Tired, aching bodies were soon stretched out on the beds.

When he felt like it, Paul played the fiddle before going to sleep. The fiddle had a hypnotic effect on Don, who was about a year old. He fell asleep wherever he happened to be. One night, he fell asleep at the table while Paul was playing. His small head dropped forward on his chest and he began slowly falling to the right. We caught him before he hit the floor.

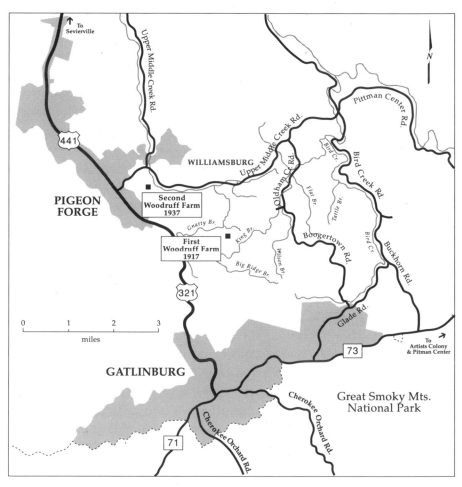

Map 10. Sevier County. Life and work in the mountains over forever,
Dorie and her family returned to the upper farm in Middle Creek.

Dorie: Woman of the Mountains

There was always a special relationship between Paul and Don. Everything Paul did, Don imitated. He shaved like Paul, he talked like Paul, he walked like Paul, and, of course, he played the fiddle like Paul. Many times I'd see them coming from the fields with Don perched like a prince on the horse's back. Every time he saw the mare, he cried to ride her.

Just after he learned to walk, he wandered away when we weren't looking. We called and called without an answer. Not knowing which way to look, we each went a different direction. I found him in the field below the garden, where we kept the mare. There he was, his arms wrapped around a front leg, trying to climb on her back. The breath went out of me. If she moved, she could kill him. She seemed to sense the position she was in. Standing very still, she waited until I pulled him away, then she jerked her head back and whirled around, galloping into the open field.

The fierce sibling rivalry Paul felt for brothers and sisters near his own age had mellowed. The hair-pulling, fist-swinging youngster was almost grown. He felt a fatherly sort of affection for the younger children. With Fred gone so much, he became a father figure to look up to and love.

Although he worked on the railroad with Pa since he was thirteen or fourteen, it never interfered with his schooling. He was almost through high school and had hopes of becoming an engineer. It was not to be, however. We were going to need his help to survive. The depression and its aftereffects left us almost penniless. Fred's work was temporary. When the power line reached Gatlinburg, he would be laid off until a new job was planned.

The isolation of the farm bothered me. There were days when we didn't see anybody but the mailman. Everybody was busy trying to make a living. If the children were unhappy, they never said anything. They were used to hard work and being by themselves.

About every two weeks, a peddler came by with his old truck full of groceries, an array of pots and pans, bran for the cows, a few dishes, and candy. We traded eggs, butter, chickens, and vegetables for sugar, flour, and, sometimes, candy. After seeing him put the chickens into the coops and then reach into the box for loose candy without washing his hands, I soon stopped the candy buying.

Wrapped candy was still in the future. Years later, a Chattanooga candy company drove me crazy with a jingle that played over and over on the radio. I can still hear it today. It goes, "Stop where you are. Buy a Brock candy bar. Brock is a dandy bar. A nickel's all you pay. B-R-O-C-K. Buy a Brock today." For now, loose, hard candy came in wooden buckets or boxes and tasted glorious to my children.

The bell on top of the Williamsburg school called the children from the hills and hollows much like the Oldham's Creek school had when I was a child. Williamsburg was still a one-room school. Not much change had taken place in this section of Sevier County. Charles and Edith went to high school in Townsend and Gatlinburg, Wayne and Dwight went the two miles to Williamsburg on foot. Flo would start to school this year. They didn't like the prospect of being burdened with a little sister. There were so many things to do, so many rocks to throw. Did they have to take her? Couldn't she wait until next year? No, I said, she was going this year, and they were to walk with her morning and afternoon.

Fred had bought her a mint-green, organdy dress and a pair of black patent-leather shoes for Easter. This was what she wanted to wear to school the first day. Not that she even wanted to go— but if it must be, then, at least, she'd look pretty.

The first day didn't work out. When the mailman came about ten in the morning, he said he'd stopped by the school and the teacher asked him to please tell Mrs. Cope to send someone to get Flo. She was crying her heart out, and it was impossible to teach above the noise.

"When I left, your little girl was out at the pump, trying to wash away her tears."

Thinking back to another time and another little girl sobbing in a one-room school in Waynesville, North Carolina, I knew what had to be done. I went to the field and signaled Paul to stop plowing and come in. He took one of the horses and started down the road to the school.

Fall flowers were making their last showing on the sides of the road. Some things had changed in the hills. The chestnut trees no longer dropped their nuts to be picked up by eager, young hands. A blight had killed them. The once proud and sought-after trees stood decaying and bug-infested. The Indians had mourned their passing most of all. Chestnuts were a source of food for mountain people. They were used in soups, stews, vegetable dishes, and desserts. Hogs raised on chestnuts produced the sweetest meat. Many hogs were fattened on them.

Midnight, the cat, gently arching and rubbing against my ankles, brought me back to the present and the problems that were with us now. Midnight was a very special cat. He had shown up one day when I was shucking corn. Sleek and black as ebony, he pleaded for my attention. I gently tossed a small ear of corn at him, and, to my surprise, he pounced on it and ate it with as much enthusiasm as he would a salmon. He loved raw corn. There were times he'd be asleep upstairs and, hearing me shucking corn outside, come to the open window and jump two floors down to get a fresh ear of corn. Cooked corn wouldn't do—it had to be milky fresh.

It wasn't long before Paul came back up the road with Flo sitting in front of him in the saddle. She didn't like the horse. Once, when coming from the field with Don and Paul, she slipped off its back and hit her head on the bridge crossing the creek. She was out cold when Paul brought her into the house. Life hadn't been easy for her, growing up with five boys. They expected her to be as tough and rambunctious as they were. Teasing her was one of their favorite games.

Reluctantly, she started back to Williamsburg the next morning. I expected to have to go get her again, but when the mailman came by, he said everything was quiet. One of the neighbors' young sons had extended a kind, understanding hand to her and made the whole thing bearable. It was a kindness she never forgot and one he probably doesn't remember. His name was Luther Brackins.

I watched our children growing up. Edith, who was going to Townsend High School, announced she wanted to marry Stanley Fox. She had known him in Tremont, where he had worked in the railroad machine shop. Stanley was the brother of Eulah Broome, the schoolteacher, and Bernice Headrick, who ran the Tremont Hotel. He was much older than Edith and was recognized as coming from one of the earliest and "best" families to settle in Sevier County. We were not surprised by her news. Stanley had shown interest in both our daughters at Tremont.

Always the practical one, Stanley had taken the trouble to look me over and interview me before he proposed to Edith. He held to the old mountain saying, "If you want to know what your wife will be like when she's old—look at her mother." I didn't realize the significance of his visit at the time when he inquired about my health and disposition. He was interested in my cooking ability and other talents I held claim to. No doubt about it, he wasn't going to take any chances this late in life.

Reverend Kurt Sutton came to our house to perform the ceremony. We all gathered in the living room. I sat in the rocking chair with Don on my lap, and the other children stood around me, wide-eyed and wondering what was going on. When the ceremony was over, I was left with five boys and one little girl. Wilma and Edith were starting their own lives apart from us. They had been born when I was so young, I felt more like their sister than their mother.

In the summer of 1938, the power line to Gatlinburg was completed. Fred came home to face life without a paycheck again. He went to work on a WPA job until his politics were questioned. When he told them he was a Republican, he was told not to report back the next day. WPA was supposed to provide work for all men regardless of their election preferences, but it became a political tool to manipulate the men chosen to work. Many men in Sevier County will remember and attest to this, while others will vehemently deny it. Political differences are never easily agreed to or resolved.

One depression job didn't seem too political. The NYA (National Youth Association) helped Paul cultivate a talent for wood-carving and helped sell his work. The eleven dollars a month from the NYA helped keep food on our table. Faithfully, he handed the money to me without keeping any for himself. He worked in Pigeon Forge and had a shop at home. Animals he had seen and loved became his models. His "ax-in-a-stump," carved from one piece of wood, attracted a lot of attention.

A lady came into the Pigeon Forge shop and asked if he could copy something from a picture. The object she wanted was an owl carved during the Italian Renaissance. He carved the owl for her and one for me. They were so good that he was asked to carve two more for a clock base. The clock was to be given to Congressman Jim Nance McCord, who later became governor.

When I looked at the delicately carved owl on the wall, I marveled at the talent and patience that had brought it out of a block of wood. Where had he learned to carve like that? He was so young and had worked so hard, there had been no time to develop fine artistic skills.

Fred and the boys raised tobacco that summer. It would bring in money for winter food and clothing and a few apples and oranges for Christmas. Late in November, they took it to the warehouse in Knoxville. Paul caught the red measles. He was over them before all the rest of us took sick. I hadn't had them, so I was in bed with six of my children.

Charles was very sick. Delirium and high fever lasted two days before his red spots appeared. Ma brewed herbs into a tea and forced it through his clenched teeth. Within hours, angry, red blotches covered him. Once the measles were on the outside, his fever went down and he slept peacefully for the first time in days. We had been so worried about Flo having any kind of illness because of her cough, left from the flu in Tremont, that we tended to neglect the others while watching for symptoms in her. However, she only had a mild case. She sat up in bed and counted the red spots on her hands and arms, complaining constantly because she couldn't get up and play. Ma finally let her up so she could take water to the rest of the fevered group.

Ma and Pa came to take care of us. Ma said she'd never seen so many people sick at the same time. She held to the idea that if measles were around, you should expose yourself or the children to them and get them over with once and for all. I had protected my children, and here we lay expecting her to look after us. It seemed to reinforce her belief that one or two in bed at a time is better than having six red-spotted, complaining folk to tend to all at the same time.

My children had all the usual childhood diseases here—mumps, measles, chicken pox, and whooping cough. The isolation of the mountains had protected them from the ordinary viruses. Croup and pneumonia were about the only things we worried about. Flu-like epidemics swept through the mountains, but measles and mumps were rare.

Christmas was miserable. None of us felt like eating or moving about. Since Mrs. Townsend had brought a new kind of Christmas to the children in the camps, we could no longer ignore it or restore it to its puritanical state of earlier days. No—Christmas was with us to stay. At times when there was no money, it caused a heaviness in the heart to see the sad faces of the children, who faced the day without games or toys. I managed to bake Fred's favorite orange cake and a chocolate cake for the children. Edith and Stanley brought Flo a doll. The boys had no gifts.

Fred was called back to the power company in the spring. This time, they promised long-term employment. We could begin to free ourselves from the tentacles of the depression that had held us in poverty. Money had been almost nonexistent. If we could get our hands on some, we knew it would have great buying power. We'd long remember that a nickel had bought a loaf of bread, a can of sardines, a can of Bruton snuff, or a big bottle of Coca Cola or Royal Crown. Carbonated beverages were known to us as "dope" in those days.

Thirty-five cents bought a blue work shirt, and ninety-eight cents bought a pair of overalls. Bacon was ten cents a pound, and a twenty-four-pound bag of flour cost fifty-five cents. Kerosene for our lamps was ten cents a gallon. So when you hear that old depression expression, "Brother can you spare a dime?" remember that ten cents bought you a pretty good meal.

The relief of having a regular paycheck was overwhelming. Pride and belief in ourselves returned. A paycheck is tangible evidence of your worth and your talents. For a man like Fred, work was essential. Since he was twelve years old, he had given a day's work for a day's pay, never asking for anything he didn't earn.

We learned there are two kinds of "tired." A man who is tired from working all day and can show something for his labor sleeps well at night. A man who is tired from working all day and whose striving produces nothing, sleeps fitfully. So, the weekly paycheck meant more than food on the table and clothes on your back. It relieved self-doubt, frustration, and despair.

With money coming in, Paul was free to return to school. He was so much older than the other boys who were graduating, the thought wasn't pleasant. Someone told him about the Alvin C. York Institute in Jamestown, Tennessee, where young people of all ages went if they needed financial assistance in completing their education. The institute had been built with money supplied by Alvin C. York, the great Tennessee hero of World War I. A movie had been made about his life, and he gave money to build the school. It was in Middle Tennessee, miles away from Middle Creek.

The prospect of having him so far away from home worried me. But he would only be gone one year, and he deserved the chance to make up the time he gave to his family. As it turned out, he was still the oldest boy graduating from Jamestown. His classmates called him "Pappy." He was the ripe old age of twenty-two.

M. L. (Marvie) Tipton, D. H. (Doc) Tipton, and Joe Murphy pose with the last log taken out of the Smokies. The establishment of the Great Smoky Mountains National Park in 1936 marked the end of an era and of a way of life.

In the spring of 1938, the last tree was cut by the Little River Lumber Company. Spruce Flats Branch was the site of the last falling tree. The end of an era had come. Once again, the mountains were silent. No trains, no skidders, no portable housing stuck on the hillside. Tiny seedlings would grow over the scars left by man. The only sounds would be rushing rivers, singing birds, and, at night, the piercing scream of the panther—just as our ancestors heard them many years ago.

The lumber companies had opened the door to the outside world. We became aware of "things"—things that money could buy, things that made life easier (or harder), things to see, things

Dorie: Woman of the Mountains

to do. Our isolation had ended. They had opened a door—a door we were forced to use as an exit from our ancestral homes. Then, after the exit, the door was closed to us. We were given visitors' rights to the land—to come and look, but not to stay.

Soon we would leave this place of rolling hills and sturdy oak, too. Fred wanted us in Knoxville with him. I had to wait for the birth of our ninth child before we left the shadows of the hazy, blue mountains.

On October 3, 1939, our daughter, Sylvia Jeane, was born. Sylvia wasn't a mountain name. I had read a story with Sylvia as the heroine. It was a beautiful name for a beautiful daughter. Ironically, Dr. Bruce Montgomery delivered her. Fred had walked to Gatlinburg to get him to come. He had delivered my first two babies, high in the Smokies. And, I suppose, it was appropriate that he deliver the last one born in the foothills.

In 1939, we left Middle Creek for the last time. It had been a refuge in times of trouble—a place we knew we could return to if our hopes and dreams faded and fate dealt cruelly with us. It was there, nestled in the rounded hills, waiting.

Epilogue

My parents, Fred and Dorie, left Middle Creek and lived in Pigeon Forge until their tenth child was born. Fredrick Phillip was born July 3, 1941. Dr. John Ogle came to our house to deliver him. We were taken to my grandparents' home on Middle Creek, blissfully ignorant of the event about to take place. Mother never told us a new baby was expected, and we never suspected a thing except that she had gained a little weight.

Fredrick Phillip was the most beautiful baby I'd seen. My joy was not shared by my sister, Jeane, who was the baby at the time. Great tears ran down her cheeks as she sobbed, "I wish that old baby hadn't come." She thought the doctor had brought him in his little black bag and could come and take him back.

In 1943, we moved to Knoxville into the first home my parents ever owned. The house was so new that it was still littered with bits of lumber, nails, and fiberboard, and smelled of paint and plaster. Carpenters were working all around us, keeping up with the building boom. Houses sprang up like mushrooms in the fields still growing corn stalks. Actually, the houses were being built for workers at Oak Ridge and the "Manhattan Project" but we didn't know that.

We caused quite a sensation the day we moved into the neighborhood. There we were—six kids in a car, Charlie Benson's truck full of assorted furniture, and a cow bawling her displeasure in Bud Beck's pickup truck. We tied the cow to the telephone pole in the corner of the yard. We had arranged to pasture her nearby, but first we had to get ourselves moved in.

For the time being, the cow would have to stay in the front yard. To make matters worse, a railroad ran through a field across the road, and every time a train went by, she bawled and fertilized the yard. We could see curtains move slightly in the houses around us. We knew all eyes were turned in our direction.

Our neighbors were from Grainger, Union and the back forty acres of Knox County, but we were "hillbillies" of recent vintage and, therefore, viewed with alarm—probably with thoughts like "Well, there goes the neighborhood!" Children gathered across the road and stood in tight little groups watching every move. If one of us walked toward them, they scattered in all directions.

Dwight started clearing the garden in the back. He was digging and sweating when he heard someone yell, "Farmer, hey, Farmer!" At first he ignored it. After a while, it grated on his nerves. He looked at the yelling boy and started toward him. The boy ran for his house and slammed the door behind him. The next day, we discovered that the family across the road was named Farmer. They had a son who was friends with the boy who yelled. He had been calling his friend, with no thoughts of slurring Dwight's background.

The transition from hillbilly to suburbanite didn't take long. Of course, there were adjustments to make, but a whole new world was waiting to be explored. Mother took several homemaking courses with the University of Tennessee Extension Service. She was an instant success with the home demonstration club because of her many talents. The natural shyness of the mountain woman was the most difficult problem she had to face. Her quiet reserve was sometimes misunderstood in a neighborhood full of coffee-klatching women.

My Father built power lines into the surrounding counties. He brought several of his old logging buddies to Knoxville to work with him. After completing the required educational background, he became a Methodist minister. He was pastor of the Ebenezer

Methodist Church in Concord and, later, the University Avenue Methodist Church in Knoxville until his death in July 1961.

We brought him back to Pigeon Forge for burial. He rests a few feet away from my Grandfather and Grandmother Woodruff. In the distance, the pale outlines of the Smokies reach upward. Giant thunderhead clouds rise slowly from the mountains and shine, pure and white, like down from angel wings. This is an ideal resting place for an old mountaineer who wanted beauty, freedom, and simplicity in his life.

Life was not easy for my parents. They came from good, healthy ancestors who were not afraid of hard work or hard times. That, too, was part of living. In their forty-seven years of marriage, they lived in two worlds. One was in a region practically unknown and unexplored, 463,000 acres of wilderness often devastated by roaring forest fires and flash floods.

The carbolic acid, quinine, turpentine, cockleburr cough syrup, herbs, and the odorous onion poultice have been replaced by new wonder drugs. In their lifetime, science has moved with lightning speed, producing miracles and wonders unheard of a few years ago. My mother has seen men go to the moon in less time than it took to go from one remote mountain peak to another. The terror felt when Halley's Comet streaked ominously across the sky has been replaced with awe, as orbiting satellites circle the earth and shine like stars in the night.

They both felt it had been easier to raise a family in the mountains than in the Knoxville suburbs. Peer pressure and the need to conform were problems faced by the younger children every day. In the logging camps, everyone was equal to everyone else. Poverty for one meant poverty for all; prosperity for one meant prosperity for all. Everyone was in the same boat, so to speak. Temptations confronted the younger children that were not even thought of in the mountains. Their role as parents was challenged in new ways.

Each generation is a step further away from the mountains, but, still, in each of us is a spirit that longs to soar like an eagle back to the place of our beginning, our home. In years to come, we can look back toward the Smokies and remember our heritage. Many ancestors lived, worked, and died under the smoky haze, leaving us a legacy of determination, courage, intelligence, and the knowledge that God is always near.

Afterword

by Durwood Dunn

The history of one woman, Dorie Woodruff Cope, and of her family, living in the heart of the Appalachian South during the first four decades of the twentieth century, offers a unique and instructive perspective on many themes, old and new, in the continuing debate over exactly how Appalachia differs from the rest of the South and from mainstream America. It is above all a cautionary tale because so many themes appear to be true only in a very limited sense or only for brief periods of time. The very complexity of Dorie's story, told here with appealing simplicity, calls into question many generalizations about Appalachian exceptionalism.

There is an underlying honesty in Dorie's narrative, which gives the larger portrayal of the life and times of families laboring in lumber camps during this period both authenticity and credibility. Although she is aware of the national image of Appalachia promulgated by such writers as Horace Kephart, this impression or image intrudes only peripherally in her own story, and applies mainly to razorback hogs rather than to her circle of family and friends. Dorie is painfully honest about her own shortcomings and failures: "I was a complete failure as a mountaineer," she laments at one point. The value of Dorie's story as representative of the Appalachian experience is increased not only by her honesty and insight but by the clear indication throughout the narrative that her life is typical and largely shared by neighbors and friends in each locale. Neither Dorie nor her family saw their experiences as atypical or exceptional, yet these very attitudes of close ties with extended family and friends offer an important insight into the Appalachian sense of community.

Perhaps the central Appalachian myth brought into question by Dorie's narrative is the idea of a static society, where people remain in one location or on the same family farm from one generation to the next. Dorie's childhood and later married life were characterized by frequent moves to an enormous number of locations over a large, geographically diverse area including Tennessee, North Carolina, and South Carolina. Far from wishing to remain permanently on some isolated, ancestral mountain farm, Dorie's family was motivated to move frequently in order to seek better economic opportunities in the lumber camps and cotton mills of the New South. In so doing, their motivation was the same as that of their fellow countrymen in other parts of America; only the duration and remuneration of these opportunities suffer in comparison.

Culturally and socially, Dorie's family also shared the American faith in progress. Dorie's mother early warned her that only by getting an education could she cope with the outside world, which was so rapidly changing. Dorie's life story chronicles a progression of new inventions and customs eagerly embraced: Christmas, oranges, Easter eggs, cookstoves, Sears and Roebuck catalogs, sewing machines, indoor plumbing, electricity, and automobiles. These are tangible symbols of how Dorie and her family accepted modernity, as did other Americans in the first decades of the twentieth century.

Nor were the younger people always in the vanguard of this revolution in material folk culture. Dorie's grandmother, Granny Jane, demonstrates to Dorie's mother a new, better, and much easier way of drying apples and peaches, by using the vapor from hot sulphur in a kiln carefully constructed of rock, mud, and boards. Of Granny Jane's instruction Dorie recalls, "She told Ma there was a better way." It is a memorable phrase, which might well have been Dorie's own slogan for her later married life.

Yet Dorie is not blinded by the limits or liabilities of progress.

She and her family judge each new idea, process, or product by its utility and reject what is not suited to their own needs. Such an empirical appraisal is nowhere better illustrated than in Dorie's estimation of modern medicine as represented by various new, male physicians. Of Dr. Bruce Montgomery's assistance at the birth of one of her sons, she notes with asperity, "As usual, he did nothing to relieve my discomfort." When her daughter Edith developed pneumonia and Dr. Edward W. Griffin offered only ineffective quinine tablets to keep the fever down, Dorie successfully resorted to the folk remedy of an onion poultice to save her child's life.

This sharp appraisal of the limits of modern medicine, including her condemnation of these physicians' excessive faith in "the curative powers of calomel, castor oil, and iodine," would cause Dorie to return many times to traditional folk medicines and midwives. But even in this reaction, she did not close her mind to the possibility of new and better medical assistance. With Dr. Robert Thomas at Pittman Center, for example, she discovered a fine, caring, and able physician, who could indeed ease the pangs of childbirth.

The knowledge and use of traditional skills was always contingent upon the family's immediate needs and financial condition. Some of her mother's many skills, such as weaving cloth from wool or flax, Dorie never learned. Yet whenever they had enough land for a garden or were forced to return to the farm, she was quite adept at canning and preserving food. Dorie's life and the survival of her family, like those of most Americans, were largely shaped by external economic forces. During the depression, when the family was at its lowest ebb and actually close to starvation, even these traditional skills could not save them. Like other Americans, Dorie's family then suffered from "self-doubt, frustration, and despair," resulting from chronic unemployment.

The adaptability of traditional mountain culture to change over time is thrown into interesting perspective by Dorie's recitation of her mother's borrowings from the Cherokees. During Dorie's early childhood, when the family moved to a farm neighboring the Qualla Boundary in western North Carolina, Dorie's mother learned from her new neighbors how to make Indian bean bread and chestnut dumplings. "Ma" even became friendly enough with Indian women to learn their taboos and their creation stories. Dorie's mother seemed to develop a real sense of cultural relativity, of understanding the Cherokees on their own terms and appreciating their abilities as "fine herb doctors and kind, sympathetic midwives." Such an appreciation of Cherokee culture and willingness to borrow from it shows an early pattern of adaptability not usually associated with Appalachian folkways.

Nevertheless, the strong sense of family and kinship, which is supposed to represent a major Appalachian characteristic, is ever-present in Dorie's narrative. Her parents were often the last resort to which the family could turn in times of sickness or unemployment. Although Dorie's parents always offered help generously, however, the relationship was not without friction. Dorie both needed her Ma and resented her interference. Dorie and Fred usually made occupational choices and consequent moves as a nuclear family seeking its independence. In one notable instance, Dorie issued an ultimatum to prevent her husband's family from persuading him to move back to North Carolina to raise chickens. Dorie's independence from her husband's relatives and her occasional friction with her own kinfolk thus strike a peculiarly modern note and suggest family relationships in transition, rather than fixed or frozen.

Dorie's role in Appalachian society as a woman is also difficult to assess accurately. She was clearly caught in a traditional patriarchy, where her role as wife and mother was predetermined by the arrival of numerous babies. Yet within the confines of her time and circumstances, Dorie, like her mother before her, was a strong woman who usually got her own way. She was fortunate to have both a father and husband who were supportive and loving, and she did not seem particularly conscious or resentful of the limitations imposed by society on women. She began voting soon after the Nineteenth Amendment passed and eagerly listened with the rest of her family to presidential candidates' campaign speeches on a battery radio.

Dorie missed her own mother when living some distance from her, yet she does not seem to have needed a network of women friends outside her own family. Her daughter recalls that when Dorie lived in a Knoxville suburb in later years her quiet reserve and natural shyness were "sometimes misunderstood in a neighborhood full of coffee-klatching women," Like Gertie Nevels in Harriette Arnow's *The Dollmaker*, Dorie is a strong woman, capable of great resourcefulness at a moment's notice. She demonstrates these qualities, for example, when she pours a kettle of boiling water on an angry bull that has been threatening her children and home. She is unlike Gertie, however, in her ability to successfully defy her husband and his relatives in a major career decision. So, despite the restrictions placed on her by society, Dorie remains firmly in control of her family throughout the narrative.

Perhaps the single most important contribution of Dorie's narrative is her vivid description of life in the various lumber camps in the Great Smoky Mountains. Her recollections of movable houses perched precariously on steep mountainsides, steam locomotives struggling across bridged abysses, influxes of Norwegian rats, earthquakes, screaming panthers, and forest fires raging out of control give us a memorable image of the life and times in locations with such evocative names as Tremont, Sam's Creek, Stringtown, Elkmont, Peawood Hollow, Eldorado, Buckeye Flats, Smokemont, Jake's Creek, Wildcat Flats, and Mark's Cove.

Not only does she carefully describe everyday life, work, food, and habits in detail, Dorie tells us the even more important facts about life in the Little River Lumber Company camps, those having to do with social and family relationships. A broad and tolerant egalitarianism existed here, she explains, because everyone had more or less economic equality. Colonel W. B. Townsend, the company president, encouraged the families of loggers to move to these camps in order to maintain social stability and minimize fighting and drunkenness. During boom times all prospered, while during recessions all suffered equally, so that no invidious distinctions ever seemed to threaten this frontier democracy. Colonel Townsend and his wife seem paternalistic but not despotic, as when, for example, Mrs. Townsend gave a Christmas party with an appropriately decorated tree and presents for all the loggers' children.

Ironically, at the same time that Dorie and her family were living in the most remote lumber camps, they were becoming familiar with the latest consumer goods in modern America, thanks to their wages and to Sears and Roebuck and Montgomery Ward catalogs. In Dorie's own words, the lumber companies had opened the door to the outside world, ending their isolation. But then, "after the exit, the door to the mountains was closed to us." They had been given only "visitors' rights to the land—to come and look, but not to stay."

This juxtaposition of remote mountain camps and modern consumer products also affected the Copes' cultural life. Dorie and her entire family were avid readers and assuaged much of the loneliness and isolation in these mountains by reading the fiction of writers like Zane Grey and Edgar Rice Burroughs—also obtainable from the indispensable Sears and Roebuck catalogs. Thus, the active folk imagination, stimulated by the spine-chilling screams of panthers and by tales of "Punch-Out" Gilland's inability to spend a night alone in a haunted cabin for a fifty-dollar reward, was further nourished by tales of Tarzan and the wild West.

The Little River Lumber Company, which employed Dorie's husband for so many years, represented an almost stereotypical example of the exploitation of Appalachian natural resources by interests outside the region. Founded in 1901 by Philadelphia capitalists, this company was by far the most ambitious log-

Dorie: Woman of the Mountains

ging-railroad project in the Smokies. In addition to completing many miles of track, which literally had to be blasted out of a rocky gorge through which Little River coursed, the company successfully adapted steam-powered machines to the rugged conditions of the wilderness. Such almost revolutionary changes in the character of logging methods enabled the Little River Lumber Company to rapidly cut more trees farther back in the Smokies than had ever previously been possible.

As a result, during the lifetime of this company and others like it, from 1901 to 1939, over 1.5 billion board feet of lumber and thousands more feet of cords of pulp, acidwood, and other wood products were extracted from the Smokies. Such extensive and exhaustive logging was an ecological disaster, magnified through the power of modern technology, and uncontrolled by any state or national regulatory agency. The resulting damage created ideal conditions for the numerous forest fires, which Dorie describes with such vividness and pain.

In conclusion, Dorie's narrative is important because it offers one definite answer to the question frequently posed by scholars as to how aware the Appalachian people were of the natural beauty surrounding them. Throughout her life, Dorie had an almost mystical appreciation of the sights, sounds, smells, and resonance of her beloved mountains. Often, while living in remote camps, high in the Smokies, which had seldom if ever before been inhabited by humans, she was transfixed by the enormous natural beauty of the locale. The crystal spring water, rhododendron and mountain laurel, moss, wildflowers, birds, and squirrels of Mark's Cove remained indelibly fixed in her dreams and imagination. At the end of her life, she tells us, "I can feel the good, cold water in my mouth and the pure, crisp air in my lungs."

Memorable descriptions of the farms in Sevier County where she lived also abound in Dorie's writing. When her family moved away from Middle Creek for the last time in 1939, Dorie felt a deep nostalgia for this "refuge in times of trouble—a place we knew we could return to if our hopes and dreams faded and fate dealt cruelly with us." Like her homesickness when as a child she went to live with her grandparents in Waynesville in order to attend school, her inexorable grief for the Smokies would continue to haunt Dorie. Perhaps such a lifelong metaphysical attachment to and intense appreciation for a particular place does not make Dorie's story unique among American autobiographies. Indeed, her narrative is often strikingly similar in both tone and style to the life experiences recorded by other Americans living in the wilderness or on the frontier farther west. Nevertheless, this love of place remains the single most distinctive "Appalachian" characteristic in the elaborate mythology of Appalachia, which stands out so clearly here. In Flo Bush's hands *Dorie: Woman of the Mountains* exhibits an authenticity and vitality that transcend the literary descriptions and artificial contrivances that earlier writers such as Mary Noailles Murfree used to represent the complex relationship between these people and their mountains.

Tennessee Wesleyan College, 1990

Suggested Readings

Blackman, Ora. *Western North Carolina: Its Mountains and Its People to 1880.* Boone, N.C.: Appalachian Consortium Press, 1977.

Browder, Nathaniel C. *The Cherokee Indians and Those Who Came After: Notes for a History of Cherokee County, North Carolina, 1835–1860.* Hayesville, N.C.: Privately published, 1973.

Bryant, F. Carlene. *We're All Kin: A Cultural Study of a Mountain Neighborhood.* Knoxville: Univ. of Tennessee Press, 1981.

Burns, Inez E. *History of Blount County, Tennessee: From War Trail to Landing Strip, 1795–1955.* Nashville: Tennessee Historical Commission, 1957.

Bush, Florence Cope. *Ocona Lufta Baptist: Pioneer Church of the Smokies, 1836–1939.* Knoxville: Misty Cove Press, 1989.

Campbell, Carlos C. *Birth of a National Park in the Great Smoky Mountains.* Knoxville: Univ. of Tennessee Press, 1960.

Campbell, Carlos C., William F. Hutson, and Aaron J. Sharp. *Great Smoky Mountain Wildflowers.* 4th ed. Knoxville: Univ. of Tennessee Press, 1960.

Catlin, David T. *A Naturalist's Blue Ridge Parkway.* Knoxville: Univ. of Tennessee Press, 1984.

Cope, Robert F., and Manley W. Wellman. *The Coutry of Gaston: Two Centuries of a North Carolina Region.* Gastonia, N.C.: Gastonia Historical Society, 1961.

Cunningham, Rodger. *Apples on the Flood: The Southern Mountain Experience.* Knoxville: Univ. of Tennessee Press, 1987.

Dorgan, Howard. *Giving Glory to God in Appalachia: Worship Practices of Six Baptist Subdenominations.* Knoxville: Univ. of Tennessee Press, 1987.

Dunn, Durwood. *Cades Cove: The Life and Death of a Southern Appalachian Community, 1818–1937.* Knoxville: Univ. of Tennessee Press, 1988.

Eller, Ronald D. *Miners, Millhands, and Mountaineers: Industrialization of the Appalachian South, 1880–1930.* Knoxville: Univ. of Tennessee Press, 1982.

Finger, John R. *The Eastern Band of Cherokees, 1819–1900.* Knoxville: Univ. of Tennessee Press, 1982.

Gaventa, John. *Power and Powerlessness: Quiescence and Rebellion in an Appalachian Valley.* Urbana: Univ. of Illinois Press, 1980.

Goehring, Eleanor E. *Tennessee Folk Culture: An Annotated Bibliography.* Knoxville: Univ. of Tennessee Press, 1982.

Greve, Jeanette S. *The Story of Gatlinburg.* 1931. Reprinted Maryville, Tenn.: Bravos Printing Company, 1976

Gunn, John C. *Gunn's Domestic Medicine.* 1830. Facsimile reprint. Knoxville: Univ. of Tennessee Press, 1986.

Inscoe, John C. *Mountain Masters, Slavery, and the Sectional Crisis in Western North Carolina.* Knoxville: Univ. of Tennessee Press, 1989.

Kane, Harnett T. *The Southern Christmas Book.* New York: David McKay, 1958.

Kenzer, Robert C. *Kinship and Neighborhood in a Southern Community: Orange County, North Carolina, 1849–1881.* Knoxville: Univ. of Tennessee Press, 1988.

Kephart, Horace. Our Southern Highlanders: *A Narrative of Adventure in the Southern Appalachians and a Study of Life among the Mountaineers.* 1913. Reprint. Knoxville: Univ. of Tennessee Press, 1976.

King, Duane H., ed. *The Cherokee Indian Nation: A Troubled History.* Knoxville: Univ. of Tennessee Press, 1979.

Lambert, Robert S. "Logging on Little River, 1890–1940." *East Tennessee Historical Society Publications* 33 (1961): 32–42.

Lewis, Helen M., Linda Johnson, and David Askins, eds. *Colonialism in Modern America: The Appalachian Case.* Boon, N.C.: Appalachian Consortium Press, 1978.

Linzey, Alicia, and Donald W. Linzey. *Mammals of Great Smoky Mountains National Park.* Knoxville, Univ. of Tennessee Press, 1971.

MacColl, Ewan, and Peggy Seeger. *Travellers' Songs from England and Scotland.* Knoxville: Univ. of Tennessee Press, 1971.

McDonald, Michael J., and William Bruce Wheeler. *Knoxville, Tennessee: Continuity and Change in an Appalachian City.* Knoxville: Univ. of Tennessee Press, 1983.

McKinney, Gordon B. *Southern Mountain Republicans, 1865–1900: Politics and the Appalachian Community.* Chapel Hill: Univ. of North Carolina Press, 1978.

Montell, William Lynwood. *The Saga of Coe Ridge: A Study in Oral History.* Knoxville: Univ. of Tennessee Press, 1970.

Pope, Liston. *Millhands and Preachers: A Study of Gastonia.* New Haven: Yale Univ. Press, 1970.

Shapiro, Henry D. *Appalachia on Our Mind: The Southern Mountains and Mountaineers in the American Consciousness.* Chapel Hill: Univ. of North Carolina Press, 1978.

Sharp, Cecil J. *English Folk Songs from the Southern Appalachians*. London: Oxford Univ. Press, 1932.

Stupka, Arthur. *Trees, Shrubs, and Woody Vines of Great Smoky Mountains National Park*. Knoxville: Univ. of Tennessee Press, 1964.

Swan, M. L. *The New Harp of Columbia*. Introduction by Dorothy D. Horn, Ron Petersen, and Candra Phillips. Facsimile ed. Knoxville: Univ. of Tennessee Press, 1978.

Thornborough, Laura. *The Great Smoky Mountains*. Revised ed. Knoxville: Univ. of Tennessee Press, 1962.

Whisnant, David E. *All That Is Native and Fine: The Politics of Culture in an American Region*. Chapel Hill: Univ. of North Carolina Press, 1983.

Appendix 1

The following names were listed in the time books belonging to Robert Vance Woodruff. They worked with the Little River Lumber Company beginning in the spring of 1923 and ending in the fall of 1934.

W. A. Rose
Jim Sanders
Horace Oakley
Marshall Reagan
E. J. Marley
Eddy Clabo
Herbert Watson
Pink Parton
Asher Watson
Elmer Metcalf
Howard Woodward
H. J. Frainkler
H. O. Marson
C. H. Starky
Grover Webb
J. D. Burnett
John Simms
Dock Ogle
Cleo McFalls
Bob Green
Luther Woodruff
C. H. Parton
James Steadman
Jim Huskey
Charles Kirby
Don Huskey
C. C. Oliver
Paul Cope
Ross Lawson

Joe Stalleon
Taylor Price
J. C. Watson
Carl Fox
Eli Brackens
Ramer Brackins
M. V. Myers
Ulyss Wilson
Dallas Ogle
Fred Cope
John Brackens
Histon Lawson
Roy Blalock
Oda Wilson
W. T. Moore
Horace Trentham
L. E. Moore
Ben Wilson
Otha Mathis
Eskel Ogle
J. L. Whaley
Lee Garland
Hugh Whaley
G. W. Wilson
Bill Shults
Henry Ogle
Jim Ogle
H. E. Ownby
Joe Cooper

J. W. Ownby
Lee Ogle
Elmer Fish
W. A. Cotter
Les Proffitt
J. H. Shults
Bill Messer
W. R. Wilson
Jack Proffitt
Gar Barns
Ben Barns
C. L. Ogle
Walt Pritchett
Yeary King
Carley Rains
Jim King
Sam Parton
Willy Whaley
Jake Parton
Otha Russell
Wesley Ogle
Bill Cooper
Garland Ogle
Eli Cooper
Howard Green
Dillard Ownby
C. R. Sutton
Pinkney Bradley
Isaac Stinnett

Marshall Ownby
John Price
Ensley Ownby
E. E. McFalls
Oliver Whaley
J. Y. Barns
Horace Barns
Milas Whitten
Dewey Williams
Kinsey Whitten
Avery Ogle
Beecher Huskey
Clyde McCarter
James McCarter
Thomas Ownby
Troy Price
Walter Gray
Ralph Kidd
Tommy Tipton
France Bradley
Alden McCarter
Forester McCarter
Jesse Shults
Lee Noland
C. O. Lesco
Jack Darco
Bedford Shults
L. D. Green
Ed Sutton
Joe Fancher
Willy Price
Lloyd Price
Clifford Price
Omar Huskey
John Ware
Newell Romines
Brad Myers
Bill King
Clyde Stratton
Bige Maples
Bill Powell
Harrison Williams
Charlie Brackens
J. H. Williamson
Henry Stricklin

Haze Tipton
Harrison Whaley
J. H. Starky
Charley Whaley
Luther Hembree
Luther Williams
Vic Shults
Houston Patty
A. L. Wilson
Hubert Markhem
Dallas Townsend
J. A. Copeland
Dallas Smith
Milas Ogle
J. M. Treadway
W. L. Connely
Ellis Myers
Joseph Carver
J. W. Watson
Denton Rayfield
Jack Parton
Arthur Hurst
Milas Gray
Hershel Brackens
Robert Blevins
Clyde Buchanan
Alia Myers
Hubert Webb
H. H. Tipton
W. E. Hedrick
Mayford Huskey
Earl Birchfield
Lee Morgan
Henry Kirkland
Paul Ogle
Oda Franklin
J.C. Brymer
J. C. Brewer
Wes Franklin
Dallas Ownby
Millas Green
Henry Noland
Earl Newman
Oliver Parton
Jabe Tipton

Wes Rayfield
Lance Huff
Houston Ball
C. H. Sparky
W. P. Parton
Benny Whaley
Garlin Ogle
Kenneth Ownby
Yonley Brackens
E. Tommy Williamson
Walt Myers
Raymond Seabolt
Dall Watson
Wade Wilson
Yeary Melton
Carl Melton
Russell Morgan
Alford Fry
Tresse Rayfield
Von Lindsey
Robert F. Cope
Loy Myers
D. A. Franklin
J. C. Gilland
Shan Tester
Ed Cook
Oliver Rayfield
Woodrow Wilson
Sam Maples
T. B. Breeden
N. M. Spradlin
Robert Ramsey
Harrison Parton
Roy Lindsey
Beecher Townsend
Bob Gray
Hugh Lawson
Wade Ownby
J. B. Dockery
Clyde Myers
Harry Rathbone
Cark Sanders
Luther Miller
Otha Henry
James Walker

Dorie: Woman of the Mountains

Appendix 2

Friends and neighbors on the logging job:

Arthur and Lura Hurst (railroad)
Henry Strickland (railroad)
Tom and Martha Moore (railroad)
Sam and Elgie Maples (railroad)
Martha Carver and Lytha McMahan (boarding house)
Pete McCarter (skidder)
Shirley and Eulah Broome, (train engineer; schoolteacher)
George Rayfield (timber cutter)
Dock Shults (railroad)
Harrison Cardwell (timber cutter)
Homer Bradshaw (clerk in company store)
Nip Cogdill (timber cutter)
Sam Henry (bookkeeper, postmaster)
George Shults (timber cutter)
Beecher Wilson (train engineer)
Jim Wilson (skidder engineer)
Mitchell Wilson (foreman on railroad)
Ernest and Bernice Headrick (ran Tremont Hotel)
Stanley Fox (machine shop)
William (Bill) Maples (machine shop)
Baus Ownby (timber cutter)
Everett and Rhella Cole (skidder)
Walter and Beadie Cole (skidder)
Alex Cole (skidder)
Henry Ogle (railroad)
Ora Townsend (skidder)

A. B. Townsend (skidder)
Dowe Townsend (skidder)
Nadine Townsend
Vida Reagan
Laura Rayfield
Reva Wilson
Tinnie Wilson Price (all friends of my daughters)
Pinkney Ownby (Baptist preacher, skidder)
Dave and Linda Gray (skidder)
Harrison Watson (railroad)
Mr. and Mrs. Eli Ownby (skidder)
Commodore Gilland (skidder)
Leonard (Punch-Out) Gilland (timekeeper)
Newt Ownby (bookkeeper)
Jim Sanders (railroad)
Eldina Wilson (friend)
Charles Brackens (railroad, skidder)
Otha Ownby (railroad)
Herbert Watson (railroad)
Horace Threntham (train)
Bob Headrick (loader)
Moses Moore (timber cutter)
Eskel Ogle (railroad)
Avery Ogle (railroad)
Avery Cogdill (timber cutter)
Harrison Williams (railroad)
Oliver Rayfield (railroad)
Wesley Rayfield (railroad)
Clyde Huskey (choker hooker)
Lofton Ownby (choker hooker)
Clarence Tinker (timber cutter)
Richard Whaley (railroad)
Arthur Whaley (railroad)
Frank Rhinehart (railroad)
Mr. and Mrs. Beecher Townsend (railroad)
Arlie Maples (railroad)
Bill Maples (machine shop)